OSAMA BIN LADEN

A Biography

OSAMA BIN LADEN

A Biography

Thomas R. Mockaitis

GREENWOOD
AN IMPRINT OF ABC-CLIO, LLC
Santa Barbara, California, Denver, Colorado, Oxford, England

PENTAGON SECURITY INTERNATIONAL
AN IMPRINT OF PENTAGON PRESS

Osama bin Laden: A Biography / Thomas R. Mockaitis

ISBN 978-81-8274-547-6

First Indian Edition 2011

Osama bin Laden, by Thomas R. Mockaitis, was originally published in hard cover by Greenwood, an imprint of ABC-CLIO, LLC, Santa Barbara, CA. Copyright © 2010 by Thomas R. Mockaitis. Hard cover edition by arrangement with ABC-CLIO, LLC, Santa Barbara, CA.

Published in India by
PENTAGON SECURITY INTERNATIONAL
An Imprint of
PENTAGON PRESS
206, Peacock Lane, Shahpur Jat
New Delhi-110049

Printed at
Syndicate Binders, A-20, Hosiery Complex, Phase II, Noida-201305.

This edition is for sale in Indian Subcontinent only.

To Martha and to my students and readers,
who make these endeavors worthwhile

CONTENTS

PREFACE

People love villains almost as much as they love heroes. Nothing satisfies discontent so much as having a fiend to vilify, an embodiment of all that is wrong with the world. Osama bin Laden is such a man. Since 9/11 he has become the most infamous man in the Western world, the demon upon whom commentators and ordinary people heap their anger like Captain Ahab with Moby Dick. For generation born and raised during the Cold War, the man fills a gap created by the collapse of the Soviet Union. Al-Qaeda terrorism and its notorious leader have replaced the Communist bogie man.

As much as we may hate Osama, however, we do not understand him. Readers of this book will be surprised to learn how little is really known outside of his family in Saudi Arabia about this well known figure. His childhood is poorly documented, as are large segments of his adult life. His family has remained understandably reticent about discussing him. Friends and acquaintances have offered recollections and reflections, but these accounts are incomplete and colored by the intervening years. Osama's own statements provide additional information, but these statements were intended to create a well groomed public persona. What can be assembled from this fragmentary evidence is the shadowy image of a life, the somewhat cleared image of an organization, and the clear outlines of a broad ideological movement. In this political biography, I have tried to bring all three dimensions together.

As with any work of this sort, I owe considerable thanks to many people. DePaul University continues to support and encourage my work, as do my colleagues in the counter-terrorism program at the Center for Civil-Military Relations at the Naval Postgraduate School. My family, especially my wife of almost thirty years, remain my greatest source of strength and energy for these projects.

INTRODUCTION

HISTORY AND THE INDIVIDUAL

Biography no longer enjoys the privileged place in historical writing it once did. Thomas Carlyle's "Great Man" theory has been debunked as the history of "dead white males." Social history has also moved the profession away from study of individuals. Celebrated by its supporters as "history without wars or presidents," and parodied by its critics as "pots and pans history," social history focuses on broad trends rather than pivotal events and on social movements instead of political leaders. Nineteenth-century Russian novelist Leo Tolstoy foreshadowed this intellectual trend. In his epic novel, "War and Peace" Tolstoy soberly assessed the limits of individual human agency in shaping events. In his description of Borodino he cast Napoleon as the self-deluded commander who believed he could actually control the unfolding battle, while the more realistic Russian General Kutuzov deployed his troops and then put his feet up on a barrel and went to sleep, realizing his powerlessness to control what would unfold in the coming hours. Borodino was a microcosm of the historical process.

Like Tolstoy, social historians rightly remind us that even the most powerful individuals have far less ability to shape events than previously imagined. Modern states and societies have proven remarkably resistant to change by individuals, no matter how authoritarian. Napoleon did not fundamentally change France. Following thirty years of brutal tyranny under Joseph Stalin, Russia remained more Russian than communist. Americans awake the Wednesday after each presidential election to a world unchanged by the "momentous" event of the night before. The president elect will enter the White House to discover his ability to deliver on a host of campaign promises far more limited than he expected.

Then there is the long-standing question of whether individuals shape events or whether events call forth individuals. Sir Isaac Newton and Gottfried Wilhelm Leibnitz invented calculus at virtually the same time and independent of one another. William Wallace published his theory of evolution shortly after Charles Darwin and completely independent of him. These "coincidences" suggest that the times bring forth "great individuals" at least as often as individuals shape the times in which they live. Centuries of scientific discovery made the world ripe for an Albert Einstein, the argument goes. If he had not put forth the theory of relativity, someone else would have. Disillusionment with decades of Democratic presidents made the election of a president like Ronald Reagan very likely. If he had not emerged as the party choice in 1980, the Republicans would have found someone very much like him. A similar statement could be made about the election of Barack Obama in 2008.

These factors, combined with growing interest in humanity below the level of the rich and powerful, led the rise of social history, which looks for the underlying social structures and broad trends that provide the continuity beneath the rapid sweep of political events and examines how these structures change over time.

THE ENDURING POWER OF BIOGRAPHY

As valuable as the social history movement has been, it does not quite satisfy as a comprehensive theory of history. According to its inexorable logic, Adolf Hitler, Winston Churchill, and Franklin Roosevelt did not matter, a conclusion that defies common sense and the experience of those who lived through the Great Depression and the Second World War. Social history has provided a necessary corrective to the distortions of the Great Man approach, but it has not displaced study of political events and the individuals who shape them. Wars and presidents still matter, even if they cannot be understood without an awareness of pots and pans.

Biography still contributes to our understanding of history and continues to enjoy a prominent place on bookstore shelves. Readers often find it easier to relate to the life of an individual than to a broad history of an era. However, today historians write biographies differently than they did a century ago. As much as they recreate an individual life, they also use that life as a window into the times in which that individual lives. By contextualizing the subject's life, the historian strikes a balance between event history and social history.

THE HISTORIAN'S CRAFT

History will never be a science in the manner of biology or chemistry. Validity in those natural sciences consists in the ability to obtain from observation and experimentation results that other researchers can replicate. Historians can never exercise such control over their subjects of their research. They do, however, try to follow the scientific method as much as possible. Like any researcher an historian begins with a question. He/she reads what has already been written on their subject to focus that question and eventually formulates a tentative response, an hypothesis. The historian then conducts further research to test the hypothesis. He or she then publishes his or her conclusions as articles in professional journals or as books. These published works become part of the body of literature on a particular subject. Other scholars read these published works while doing their own research. They rebut, qualify, or extend the original conclusion, thus continuing the process of historical inquiry.

THE CHALLENGE OF SOURCES

In reconstructing the past historians are at the mercy of the evidence that has survived. The most interesting historical questions cannot be answered without documents. Those documents were usually written for practical purposes in their own time, not to inform future historians. King Hammurabi's Code from ancient Babylon has survived but not court records from his reign, assuming such records were even kept. We know the penalty the law giver laid down for various crimes, but we cannot determine how often people committed these crimes or how frequently and severely they were punished. The historical record is always frustratingly fragmentary and incomplete. The farther back in time the historian looks, the more this problem arises, but even for contemporary figures, it never completely disappears.

FINDING BIN LADEN

For a contemporary figure of such notoriety, Osama bin Laden is surprisingly elusive. Not only does he elude capture, but he also defies understanding. The record of his life is very fragmentary. Few available documents record his childhood. Even the exact month and day of his birth are not part of the public record. His early life must be reconstructed from the eyewitness accounts of those who knew him as he grew up in Saudi Arabia. What he did on 9/11 may unavoidably color their recollections. Presumably his family knows a great deal more about him than they are willing to say. Since he became a terrorist, his relatives have maintained a closely kept conspiracy of silence about Osama.

Once bin Laden publically took up the cause of jihad, the trail of documents became richer. He made numerous pronouncements about the ideology he espoused, his goals and objectives. However, by then he belonged to an organization and a movement. His role as the leader or perhaps only the titular head of al-Qaeda make it difficult to determine whether he was speaking for himself or his movement. Even when his fame (or infamy) was at its height, from 1996 to the present, he produced very few documents by his own hand. As the leader of a clandestine organization, he granted few interviews and then did so only under tightly controlled circumstances. Reconstructing his personal life has been and will probably always remain a great challenge.

THE ISSUE OF PERSPECTIVE

Historical research and writing require a certain amount of empathy. Biographers in particular try as far as possible to put themselves in the shoes of the person whom they study in order to better understand that individual. Empathy becomes very problematic, however, when the subject under study perpetrates mass murder.[1] Osama bin Laden, of course, is such a perpetrator. Besides struggling to empathize with their subjects, historians like all human beings have their opinions, beliefs, and prejudices, the components of a complex worldview that unavoidably affect their points of view and color their prose. The more an historian's own culture and society differ from his subject's, the greater the challenge of understanding will be. Recognizing these truths, however, can set one free—to a degree. Complete objectivity is impossible, but all historians strive to get as close to it as possible.

GOALS OF THIS BOOK

In writing this book I have a single purpose and a dual audience. I hope to make the most infamous man in the Western world easier to understand. This account is a political rather than a personal biography. Too little information is available on Osama bin Laden's personal life to flesh out more than a blurred image of him as a human being. It is, however, both possible and desirable to situate him within the context of his world. That task requires examining the history of Saudi Arabia in the twentieth century, during which the kingdom underwent rapid and jarring modernization, at least in the technological sense of the term. It also necessitates looking at the religion of Islam in some detail, for only by doing that can the reader learn how Islamist extremists have perverted that religion to their own violent ends.

The biographical series to which this book belongs seeks to reach students and the educated reading public. Because this book may be used as teaching tool, I have taken more time to explain the historian's craft than I would normally do in an historical monograph. The ultimate goal of any good history book or course should be to teach readers and students to use the discipline of history to better understand their world. With that in mind, I have annotated the bibliography, providing commentary on the strengths and limitations of the sources used to write this book. I have also included an appendix of primary sources, public domain documents that the reader can examine to supplement the narrative account presented in the book.

With Osama bin Laden still at large, and the implications of his deeds continuing to play themselves out, my conclusions can only be tentative.

Future historians will have more information and the advantage of hindsight. At this point in time, I can only make the best use of the evidence, however fragmentary. Fortunately, I learned from the publication of my first book almost twenty years ago that there is no such thing as thing as a definitive historical work. We all contribute to an ongoing discussion among ourselves and our readers. Good research and writing provide some answers to historical questions, but more importantly they encourage further research and writing.

NOTE

1. See, for example, Ian Kershaw, *The Nazi Dictatorship: Problems and Perspectives of Interpretation,* 4th ed. (London: Arnold/New York: Oxford University Press, 2000).

TIMELINE: EVENTS IN THE LIFE OF OSAMA BIN LADEN

1932	Abdul Aziz Ibn Saud unifies most of the Arabian Peninsula, creating the modern Kingdom of Saudi Arabia.
1948	After declaring independence, Israel defeats five Arab armies in the first Arab-Israeli War.
1956	Britain, France, and Israel collaborate in the second Arab-Israeli War. Britain regains control of the Suez Canal, and Israel seizes the Sinai Peninsula. International pressure led by the U.S. forces both countries to relinquish their gains. The following year the UN deploys the first peacekeeping mission to the Sinai.
1958	Osama bin Laden is born in Riyadh, Saudi Arabia.
1966	Sayid Qutb is executed in Egypt by President Gamal Abdul Nasser, becoming a martyr for the Islamist cause.
1967	Mohammed bin Laden, Osama's father, dies when his private airplane crashes near one of his worksites in Saudi Arabia. Osama returns from boarding school in Beirut, Lebanon and completes his education in Saudi Arabia. Israel defeats the forces of Egypt, Syria, Jordan, and Iraq in the Six-Day War. Israel gains control of the Golan Heights, Gaza, the Sinai Peninsula, and the West Bank, including East Jerusalem, which contains the Dome of the Rock, Islam's third holiest site.

1973	Israel defeats Egypt and Syria in the Yom Kippur War. American aide is crucial to the Israeli victory.
1979	Ayatollah Khomeini's Islamic Revolution triumphs in Iran. Islamist extremists seize the Grand Mosque in Mecca. Soviet Forces occupy Afghanistan to support its communist government.
1979-89	Afghan insurgents supported by covert American and Saudi aide fight a successful insurgency to expel the Soviets. Osama bin Laden joins foreign *mujahedeen* aiding the Afghan insurgents.
1984	Along with Abdullah Azzam, Osama bin Laden sets up the Afghan Service Bureau in Peshawar Pakistan. The Service Bureau supports foreign *mujahedeen* traveling to Afghanistan to fight the Soviets.
1986	Osama bin Laden forms his own group of Arab Afghan fighters and builds them a based called "the Lion's den" near the Afghan border with Pakistan.
1987	Osama bin Laden leads a disastrous raid on the Afghan town of Khost.
1988	Osama bin Laden, Abdullah Azzam, and others create al-Qaeda (the base).
1989	East Germans open the Berlin Wall, ending the Cold War.
1990	Iraqi dictator Saddam Hussein invades Kuwait and threatens Saudi Arabia. Osama bin Laden offers to form an Arab mujahedeen army to expel the invaders.
1991	An American-led coalition of 500,000 troops expels the Iraqis from Kuwait. American troops remain in Saudi Arabia after the war, angering Osama bin Laden. The Soviet Union collapses.
1992	After briefly visiting Pakistan, Osama bin Laden goes into voluntary exile in Sudan.

1993. Ramsey Yousef and the Blind Sheikh Abdul Rahman detonate a truck bomb in the basement of the World Trade Center, killing six people and wounding 1,042. U.S. Army Rangers die in Mogadishu during a failed effort to capture Somali warlord Mohammed Farrah Aidid. Al-Qaeda takes no part in the fighting, but bin Laden later praises the Somalis and foreign mujahedeen who assisted them.

1994 Saudi Arabia revokes Osama bin Laden's passport.

1996 U.S. and other states pressure Sudan to expel bin Laden. He relocates to Afghanistan and issues fatwa against Zionists and Crusaders. Hezbollah bombs the Khobar Towers in Riyadh, Saudi Arabia, killing 19 U.S. and one Saudie servicemen and wounding 372 others. Osama bin Laden issues a fatwa against "Jews and Cursaders."

1998 Osama bin Laden issues a fatwa on behalf of the World Islamic Front calling on devout Muslims to kill Americans where ever and whenever possible. In August,
Al-Qaeda operatives bomb the U.S. embassies in Darussalam, Tanzania and Nairobi, Kenya. The U.S. launches cruise missiles at al-Qaeda training camps in Afghanistan and a pharmaceutical plant in Khartoum, Sudan. The plant is mistakenly presumed to be producing chemical weapons.

2000 Al-Qaeda suicide bombers attack the destroyer U.S.S. Cole in Aden harbor, killing 19 U.S. sailors and severely damaging the vessel. U.S. government agencies foil terrorist plots timed to coincide with millennium eve celebrations (December 31, 1999), including a plan to bomb Los Angeles International Airport.

2001 On September 11, 19 al-Qaeda terrorist operating in four teams hijack four U.S. airlines. They crash two planes into the twin towers of the World Trade Center and a third into the Pentagon. Passengers struggle to recapture the fourth plane as it heads for Washington, forcing the terrorists to crash it into a field in Pennsylvania. The attacks kill 2998 along with the 19 hijackers, the worst terrorist incident in U.S. history. President George W. Bush declares a Global War on Terror. U.S. Special Operations and CIA teams backed by American air power help the Northern Alliance overthrow the Taliban in Afghanistan. A coalition of NATO forces occupies the country to support its new government led by Hamid Karzai.

2002 In March, Osama bin Laden escapes an effort to capture him during Operation Anaconda, fleeing across the border with Pakistan. In November, Jemaah Islamiya, an Indonesian terrorist organization affiliated with al-Qaeda bombs a nightclub in Bali killing 202 people and wounding more than 100 others.

2003 An American led coalition invades Iraq in March under the pretext that its dictator Saddam Hussein is acquiring weapons of mass destruction and cooperating with terrorist organizations. U.S. forces reach Baghdad in a few weeks. The end of conventional operations is followed by a growing insurgency against the coalition and its Iraqi supporters. On November 21, Martyr Abu-Hafs al-Misri Brigades bombed two synagogues in Istanbul, Turkey. Five days later they bombed the HSBC bank and the British Consulate. The attacks kill 57 people and would over 700.

2004 On March 11, the Abu Hafs al-Masri Brigade, an al-Qaeda affiliate, bombs commuter trains and a train station in Madrid, Spain killing 191 people and wounding over 600 others. The insurgency in Iraq escalates and is exacerbated by conflict between Shi'a and Sunni Muslims.

2005 On July 7, four terrorists detonate backpack bombs in the London transit system. Three of the terrorists bomb Underground trains and a fourth detonates his bomb on a bus. The attacks kill 52 people and wound more than 770 others. On July 21, four more terrorists attempt to bomb the London Underground. The attack fails because the bomb detonators fail to set off the main charges. British security forces apprehend the terrorists and their support cell.

2006 British authorities foil an al-Qaeda plot to blow up airplanes over the Atlantic, apprehending 26 suspected terrorists. U.S. casualties in Iraq exceed 3000, more than the total number who died on 9/11. The security situation in Afghanistan deteriorates as a revitalized Taliban and al-Qaeda carry out widespread attacks from safe havens in Pakistan. A bipartisan report on the Iraq War is scathingly critical of the U.S. campaign. The White House announces its "Surge" strategy, promising to increase U.S. troop strength by 30,000, appointing General David Petraeus to command U.S. forces in Iraq. The Anbar Awakening enlists support of local Iraqi leaders in an effort to defeat foreign terrorists operating in the country and to quell the insurgency. An American bombing raid kills al Abu Musab al-Zarchawi, leader of al-Qaeda in Iraq.

2007 Al-Qaeda uses medical doctors in an abortive plot to bomb London nightclubs. Crudely made car bombs fail to detonate. One terrorist attempts to drive through the barricade protecting a terminal at Glasgow airport with a car bomb. He is badly burned in the attempt, but no one else is injured.

2008 In November Laskar'i'taiba, a Pakistani-based terrorist organization trained by al-Qaeda attacked hotels and restaurants in Mumbai, India. President Barack Obama is elected President of the U.S., promising to withdraw American troops from Iraq and refocus efforts on defeating a resurgent Taliban and al-Qaeda in Afghanistan.

2009 President Obama announces a timetable for withdrawing combat troops from Iraq, agreeing to leave support troops in place for some time afterwards. He announces that reinforcements will be sent to Afghanistan. In June, Pakistani forces begin an offensive against the Taliban in the Swat Valley. In July, 4000 U.S. Marines in cooperation with Afghan government forces conduct an offensive to clear Helmond Province of the Taliban.

2011 A half hour after midnight on Monday, May 2, 2011, two helicopters deployed twenty-five members of S.E.A.L. (SEA-Air-Land) Team 6, the Navy's elite counter-terrorism force, to a compound in Abbattobad, Pakistan. The team stormed its main building and in a second-story bedroom they shot and killed the world's most wanted man. Osama bin Laden was fifty-four years old. He had spent much of the previous decade in hiding, perhaps living as much as five years of it in the comfortable compound with members of his family under the nose of the Pakistani Army, whose military academy stands nearby. Although the White House decided against releasing photos of the dead terrorist leader for fear of inflaming the passions of his supporters, no serious observer questioned his death. A few days after the raid, al-Qaeda confirmed that its founder was gone.

CHAPTER 1

OSAMA THE MAN

Osama bin Laden is an elusive man. Not only has he evaded capture by the most powerful nation on earth for over a decade, he has also (albeit unintentionally) confounded efforts by biographers to reconstruct significant segments of his life. Despite his infamy, we know relatively little about Osama as a man, especially during the formative years from birth to age twenty-one. This dearth of information about the al-Qaeda leader's childhood and youth stems from the nature of his homeland. Saudi Arabia in the 1960s and 1970s was a land in rapid transition. Oil profits had made the royal family and those around them enormously wealthy while leaving many Saudis largely unaffected by the prosperity. Illiteracy rates remained high and the country's infrastructure under-developed. The process of state formation, which had unfolded across several centuries in Western Europe had yet to be completed. The institutions of central government did not function as fully as those of many other states. The disinclination of Saudi Arabia's predominant Wahhabi sect of Islam to celebrate birthdays or encourage photographs also made the record of Osama's life thinner than it might otherwise have been.

The nature of Saudi Arabia resulted in a dearth of the documents historians rely upon for research. Osama has no birth certificate, for example.

In the absence of such official records, biographers rely on interviews. Bin Laden has granted a handful of these, all of them after he had founded al-Qaeda. While these interviews provide useful information on his worldview and intentions, they shed little light on the early years of his life. Osama has said little about his early years, and when he did comment on them, he interpreted events through a theological lens. Like most ideologies, he also reads his own history backwards, insisting that he consistently held views that evidence shows took years to evolve. Family members, friends, and acquaintances have provided some information on Osama, but their testimony must be viewed with a healthy skepticism, especially since most of it was garnered after 9/11. The bin Ladens have good reason to distance themselves from the family black sheep, while friends and acquaintances might be tempted to embellish. The memories of all who knew him over the years are prone to editing and omission. Given Osama's legendary shyness, many who knew him can offer little more than impressions.

Because of the shortage of documents and the limitations of interviews and recollections, biographers must speculate about key aspects of bin Laden's childhood and youth. They rely heavily on knowledge of the society in which he grew up to frame their narrative. From this context and what concrete information exists they conjecture about the formative events in his life. The deeper one delves into the man's psychological development, however, the more speculative such conjecture inevitably becomes.

SAUDI ARABIA

The country in which bin Osama bin Laden was born and raised is an ancient land but a very new state. In 1905, the Arabian Peninsula consisted of numerous principalities and Bedouin tribes. Two power centers dominated the lands that would become modern Saudi Arabia. In the west, the Hashemite family ruled a costal strip encompassing the holy cities of Mecca and Medina and the city of Jeddah. In the northeast, Abdul Aziz Ibn Saud controlled the region around Riyadh. During the First World War, the British backed the Hashemite rebellion against the Ottoman Turks, but after the war they changed sides. At the 1920 Cairo Conference led by Secretary for War and Air Winston Churchill the British decided to back Ibn Saud. Saud swiftly expanded his rule, conquering the Jebel Shammar in 1921, Mecca in 1924, and Medina in 1925. In 1932, he renamed his new kingdom Saudi Arabia. Ibn Saud had risen to power by harnessing the religious zeal of warrior Wahabi Bedouins known as the Ikwhan. Once he consolidated power, however, Saud had to repress these zealots in order to modernize the country.

Since most of the kingdom was barren desert, the European colonial powers cared little who ruled it. The situation changed dramatically with the discovery of oil in the 1930s. Beneath kingdom lay the largest reserves of the twentieth-century's most valuable strategic resource. In every other respect, however, Saudi Arabia was a backward country, which had to rely on foreign engineers, businessmen, and other experts to extract petroleum and manage its refinement and sale. Unfortunately, Abdul Aziz and his successors spent most of the oil revenue on building palaces and living the high life than they did in building infrastructure or improving the lives of ordinary Saudis. This situation did not change significantly until the 1960s, the years of Osama bin Laden's boyhood.[1]

Saudi Arabia's wealth and rapid, if uneven, modernization created a disturbance felt throughout the Arab world but which particularly disturbed the conservative desert kingdom. With the Western technical expertise, which the Saudis desperately needed, came Western influence and culture, which they did not want and deeply resented. Oil wealthy catapulted a largely medieval kingdom from the Middle Ages into the twentieth century with wrenching force. The transition produced deep tensions between a desire to preserve the kingdom's conservative way of life and its need to modernize. This tension would produce a conservative Islamic movement known as Islamism. An extreme form of this Muslim revival movement would inspire Osama bin Laden's terrorist campaign against the government of his native land and the United States, which supported it.

THE BIN LADENS

The rise of the bin Laden family to a position of unprecedented wealth and power paralleled the emergence of Saudi Arabia as a modern state Osama's father Mohammed bin Laden was born in the Hadramut region of Yemen in or around 1905. He left home in 1925 (again, the date is uncertain) and settled in Jeddah, a major city in western Saudi Arabia.

There he held menial jobs, finally settling down in the construction business, a field for which he demonstrated an aptitude. He founded his own company in 1931, according to the Bin Laden Group official history.[2] He began building houses, worked as a brick layer for the Arabian American Oil Company, and eventually secured government contracts. His ability to work both with foreign investors and the monarchy, which needed but distrusted outsiders, earned Mohammed bin Laden a fortune. Oil profits funded numerous royal palaces and the roads that connected them, which Mohammed built. His willingness to loan money to the profligate monarchs ensured that he remained in the king's good graces. Eventually bin Laden's firm received lucrative contracts to renovate the Mosque of the Prophet in Medina and the Grand Mosque in Mecca, both the center of a lucrative pilgrimage industry.

Like most wealthy Saudis, Mohammed bin Laden sired many children by numerous women. Islam allows a Muslim man up to four wives if he can provide equitably for all of them. Those men who could afford it easily circumvented the limit through the practice of serial marriage. Divorce occurs more easily and carries less of a stigma under *sharia* (Islamic law) than it traditionally has in the Christian West. Sharia does, however, require a man to provide for his former spouses. By most accounts, Mohammed bin Laden fathered 54 children by 22 wives. To his credit, he assured each of them a comfortable standard of living, in some cases far above what they had enjoyed in their families of origin. He provided them with a steady income and/or remarried them to respectable men in his employ.

When Mohammed died in a plane crash in 1967, the monarchy placed his holdings in trust. Fortunately for the family, his eldest son Salem proved as shrewd a businessman as his father. He ingratiated himself with successive Saudi monarchs and established the Saudi bin Laden Group, which he transformed from a construction company into an international holding company with diverse assets around the world. Where Mohammed was serious and devote, Salem was happy-go-lucky. However, he had inherited his father's good sense and work ethic. He managed to balance the life of an international playboy abroad with that of a serious businessman at home. When he himself died in an aviation accident in 1986, he left the bin Laden group in such good shape that his younger brother Bakr could take the helm without a hitch and continue to maintain and grow the family fortune.[3]

OUTLINE OF A LIFE

The undisputed details of Osama bin Laden's life area relatively few. He was born in Riyadh, Saudi Arabia in 1957, though the exact month is not agreed. In 1968, he attended Al Thagr High School in Jeddah. He married his first wife in 1974 and attended King Abdul Aziz University, also in Jeddah, where he studied economics but did not earn a degree.

Bin Laden's mother, Alia Ghanem, belonged to a poor Syrian family who married her at the age of fourteen to Mohammed bin Laden in 1956, when the construction magnate was in his fifties. She gave birth to Osama about a year later. Mohammed divorced her, probably soon after the boy's birth as the two had no further children together.[4] She remarried and had several more children with her new husband.

As the 17th or 18th of Mohammed's sons by a junior wife, Osama does not appear to have suffered any disadvantage or lower status in the patriarch's vast extended family, although he did live away from the bin Laden compound because of his mother's remarriage.[5] There is no evidence that her new husband mistreated the boy or that their relationship was difficult. However, as an adult Osama never mentioned him in any of his public statements. Those who knew Osama as a child and young man have also said practically nothing about his stepfather. He appears to have had little hand in raising the boy and no great influence upon him.

Saudi parents shape the lives of their children just as American parents do, although the number offspring complicates a father's relationship with his children. Born just nine years before Mohammed's death, Osama must have had limited contact with a father whose business required him to lead an itinerant life. Mohammed also had to divide what time he had for family among his 54 children. By every account, however, he was a loving if austere parent who treated his sons equally, raising them to be devout Muslims and expecting them to work at an early age. However, the shear number of his wives and children coupled with the construction projects he regularly visited throughout the kingdom probably allowed Mohammed little time with any of his children. Most interaction consisted of formal gatherings of the boys seated on the floor as the family patriarch quizzed them on the *Quran*.[6] He also took them to construction sites with him. When the boys reached adulthood, Mohammed employed them in his growing company.

As a younger son of his father's very junior wife, Osama had even less contact with his father than did his older step brothers. Mohammed bin Laden died in a plane crash in 1967. Ten-year old Osama was still at the age boys idolize their fathers, something he would continue to do his entire life. In a 1999 interview as a grown man he demonstrated both his adulation for his father and his propensity for mythic exaggeration. "It is with Allah's grace," bin Laden concluded, "that he would occasionally pray in all three mosques [in Mecca, Medina, and Jerusalem] in one day."[7] Devout though he was, Mohammed bin Laden would have been hard pressed to pull off such a feat given the distances between the mosques.

Considerably less is known about Osama's relationship with his mother. Given the seclusion of women in Saudi Arabia and their lack of political rights, her silence comes as no surprise. Osama's neighbor and childhood friend Khaled Batarfi described her as a "moderate Muslim. She watches TV." He also insists that Osama obeyed her more than any of her other children, though he refused to give up jihad, placing duty to Islam above filial devotion. He has remained in touch with her throughout his years of exile and hiding.[8] She came from a relatively poor family in Syria, who probably benefited from her marriage to the Saudi billionaire. Osama spent some time with her family, but does not seem to have been particularly attached to them.

LIFE AMONG THE BIN LADENS

Bin Laden grew up in the household of his mother away from the bin Laden compound in which most of his half brothers and sisters lived. However, by all accounts, his siblings included him in their activities. This acceptance does not seem to have changed even as Osama became more religious. Large, wealthy Saudi families tended to produce at least a couple of zealous sons, whom they tolerated and perhaps encouraged the way large Catholic families used to encourage one child to become a nun or priest. His less pious siblings no doubt found his disapproval of their dress and behavior burdensome, and he could be a wet blanket, especially at the beach.[9]

Osama bin Laden did travel abroad with other family members. In 1970 he accompanied his eldest brother Salem, the new head of the family business, on a trip to Sweden, and the following year made the same trip as part family outing, which included Salem and 22 of his siblings. Besides being very friendly, Osama made little impression on the owner of the hotel where he stayed, save for the profligate manner in which he and his brother lived. They parked their Rolls Royce on the street illegally, laughing off the daily fines, and discarded their expensive Christian Dior and Yves St. Laurent white dress shirts after one wearing. He did not, however, join his brother at the local nightclub.[10]

Bin Laden went to London at age twelve, according to a close friend, and may have made other journeys to Europe as well. By one account, Osama made one trip to the U.S. to seek medical treatment for one of his sons.[11] In the absence of corroborating medical or customs evidence, this story cannot be accepted. If by chance the trip did occur, it would have been of limited duration, giving him little real exposure to American life.

THE TRAUMAS OF CHILDHOOD

The experts have combed Osama's childhood and youth for signs of trauma or interrupted development to explain his extremist behavior as an adult. Loss of his father at such a tender age was no doubt a blow, but many children have lost parents far more involved in their lives than Mohammed bin Laden was in his. By the time Osama was old enough to be aware of his surroundings his mother had remarried, so there is no evidence that he really experienced being the only child of a single mother. Claims that Alia had been scorned by the bin Ladens as a very junior wife are unsubstantiated. She certainly enjoyed a much higher quality of life with the man to whom Mohammed married her after the divorce than she would have with any likely husband from her own community.

Assertions that bin Laden was isolated from his siblings growing up seem equally unfounded. He was a toddler when his parents divorced and naturally stayed with his mother. As he grew older, however, he spent ample time with his siblings. He may have felt isolated from them because of his different address, but there is no evidence in available records or from personal testimony to support this claim. "Osama was perfectly integrated into the family," his sister-in-law wrote in her autobiography. "He was not strikingly different from the other brothers, just younger and more religious."[12]

His mother corroborates this assessment, describing Osama as "a shy kid, very nice, very considerate. He has been always helpful. I tried to instill in him the fear and love of God, the respect for his family, neighbors and teachers."[13] His close friend Khaled Batarfi claims that bin Laden was very attached to his mother, especially after the death of his father. "She was all that there was there," he observed. "He was so obedient to her . . . maybe because he wasn't close to his father."[14] Such attachment and even life-long intimacy between a boy who had lost his father at a young age and his mother hardly seems unusual.

Any conclusions about how traumatic events might have shaped Osama bin Laden must be highly speculative.[15] Perhaps the hardest thing for Americans who witnessed the devastating attacks of 9/11 to accept is that people who become terrorists do not necessarily do so as the result of childhood trauma or some psychological pathology. While the foot soldiers of the movement still tend to come from economically and/or socially marginalized groups, the leadership usually does not. They are better educated and more affluent than those they order to die for the cause. An impressive body of scholarship on the Holocaust corroborates the conclusion that ordinary people are quite capable of extraordinary acts of cruelty and destruction under the right circumstances.[16]

EDUCATION

Mohammed bin Laden sent many of sons abroad to be educated. In the 1950s and 1960s, Saudi Arabia had few good secondary schools and hardly any institutions of higher learning. Some of the bin Laden boys attended boarding school in England, Lebanon or Syria and then went on to universities in Europe or the United States. Osama had the least exposure of any of them to foreign education. With the exception of a brief stint of less than a year in 1967 at a Quaker boarding school in Lebanon, his education took place entirely within Saudi Arabia, a fact that may have contributed to his narrowly conservative outlook.[17] He probably returned to Saudi Arabia as result of his father's death and not returned to the school. None of his school records are available to researchers, so it is difficult to reconstruct his life during the elementary years. His mother said that he was "not an A student. He would pass exams with average grades. But he was loved and respected by his classmates and neighbors."[18]

Bin Laden's high school years are better documented, although the record of this phase of his life is also incomplete. After he returned home in 1967, his mother enrolled him in Al Thaghr Model School in Jeddah, where he completed his secondary education. Like most Al Thaghr students, Osama commuted from his mother's home. Far from being a conservative Madrasa, the elite private school dressed its students in English prep school uniforms and offered a modern curriculum using western educational methods. By all accounts bin Laden was an unremarkable student. He earned average grades, was reticent to volunteer answers, but responded well when called upon. "He wasn't pushy at all," recalled his English teacher. "Many students wanted to show you how clever they were. But if he knew the answer to something he wouldn't parade the fact. He would only reveal it if you asked him."[19]

While at Al-Thaghr, bin Laden fell under the influence of a Syrian Physical Education teacher with Islamist sympathies if not direct ties to Egypt's radical Muslim Brotherhood. The young man invited Osama to join a small Islamic study group, offering sports and extra credit as incentives. The teacher exposed the boys to extremely conservative ideas, advocating a return to traditional Muslim values and the merging of politics and religion. These ideas appealed to bin Laden's conservative bent, and he soon joined the school religious committee, playing a prominent role in its activities. He grew his beard and dressed modestly, refusing to wear shorts even on the soccer field.[20]

In 1976, Osama bin Laden matriculated at Abdul Aziz University in Jeddah. There he studied economics but left after a few years without earning a degree. According to his best friend at the time, Osama was already quite religious, refusing to watch movies or listen to music, which he considered *haram* (forbidden by Islamic law). The same friend noted that he and Osama both encountered political Islam at university. They read Sayid Qutb's, *Milestones*, and *In the Shade of the Quran*. They also attended lectures by Sayid's brother Mohammed Qutb, who taught at the university.[21]

WORK

Like all his brothers, bin Laden worked in the family business. Following his father's death, the king placed Mohammed's assets in trust. Within a few years, however, Mohammed's oldest son Salem reasserted control and managed the family business until his death in 1986. An effective manager, Salem cultivated his relationship with the monarchy and so maintained the privileged position his father had acquired. Salem doled out responsibility and incomes to his brothers and sisters according to their needs and abilities. Even though they earned more than enough from company profits and investments to live comfortably, most bin Laden sons chose to work anyway.

As with so much of his life, the precise details of Osama's work history remain unclear. He recalls traveling with his father to construction sites around Saudi Arabia, but he provides no details as to which sites or how often he visited them. Osama's construction of cave complexes and camps during the Afghan war against the Soviet's and his road building in Sudan indicate that he had acquired considerable knowledge of the construction trade. Between the time he quit university and his departure for Afghanistan, he probably managed some construction projects for the family company. He seems to have adopted his father's hands-on approach to management. His close friend noted that when Osama worked with his brothers, he "used to go to the bulldozer, get the driver out and drive himself."[22]

MARRIAGE AND FAMILY

Although he revered his father, Osama bin Laden disagreed with Mohammed's practice of serial marriage, which he considered contrary to the spirit if not the letter of Islamic law. He confined himself to the four wives the Prophet allowed, since providing for all of them equally on his income would not be a problem. Like any young man with ragging hormones, he wished to become sexually active, but unlike his older brother Salem, he was not willing to have sex outside of marriage. As a result he married young. Osama was just seventeen when he wed his cousin, Najawa Ghanem, who was fourteen. According to custom, she took the name of her eldest male child Abdullah and was commonly addressed as "Umm Abdullah." "Umm" in Arabic means "mother of;" "abu" means "father of." Osama went on to marry three other women Umm Hamza, Umm Khaled, and Umm Ali. Contrary to popular belief, the conservative brand of Islam practiced in Saudi Arabia does not deny women an education or even a profession. Two of bin Laden's wives were highly educated and pursued careers of their own. Umm Hamza was a professor of child psychology, and Umm Khaled taught Arabic grammar.[23] All four women bore Osama children, with the first and youngest contributing the most. According to one reliable source he has eleven children with his first wife, one with his second, four with his third, and three with his fourth—a total of 19.[24]

Bin Laden's four wives did not share the same home. When he lived in Saudi Arabia and later Sudan, they occupied different apartments in the same building. When he moved to Afghanistan, they lived in different cottages within the same walled compound. Although the wives generally got along, tensions occasionally arose. According to Zaynab Ahmed Khadr, daughter of one of bin Laden's followers who lived in the same compound with him in Kandahar, Osama favored Umm Hamza and often confided in her. Seven years older than bin Laden, Umm Hamza, the university professor, may have had a wisdom and maturity that Osama appreciated. This attention made Umm Abdullah, his first (and therefore senior) wife, very jealous. She was three years younger than Osama, quite beautiful, but poorly educated. She and bin Laden quarreled often. He does seem to have tried to placate her as much his itinerant life would allow. For example, despite his professed hatred of western secularism, he allowed her to buy American perfume and lingerie.[25]

True to his convictions on marriage, bin Laden never initiated a divorce from any of his wives. His fourth wife, however, chose to leave him. The split took place while the entire family was living in Sudan after his Saudi citizenship had been revoked in 1994. Umm Ali and Osama had never gotten along well.[26] Separation from her family, the lower quality of life in Sudan, and the prospect of perhaps never returning to Saudi Arabia no doubt added to her unhappiness. She asked Osama for a divorce, which he granted, and she returned home with their three children. He then married a Yemeni woman who bore him at least one additional child.

In addition to avoiding divorce, bin Laden remained faithful to his wives. He never kept a concubine or resorted to sex outside marriage. Unlike some religious puritans he did not consider sex part of man's baser nature to be indulged in solely for procreation. He simply held that it belonged within marriage. He seems to have taken a bride at such an early age in order to have an acceptable outlet for his healthy sex drive. Outside the home he held scrupulously to the separation of the sexes. To avoid the temptation of lustful thoughts he would even avert his eyes when a maid entered a room.

By all accounts, Osama was a strict but loving father who spent as much time as possible with his children. He would take them into the desert on camping trips, help them with their homework, and play games and sports with them. Although he enforced his core Islamic beliefs, bin Laden indulged his children in ways that contradicted his rigid pronouncements. According to the daughter of one of his associates in Afghanistan, he allowed his daughters to listen to music, which he apparently enjoyed himself, even though he condemned it as *haram* (forbidden by Islam). He also let his sons play Nintendo.[27] This account differs sharply from that given by his sister-in-law when he lived in Saudi Arabia. She insisted that bin Laden "did not like to listen to music or to watch TV, and he prevented his children form doing so."[28] Perhaps in this one regard, the years had mellowed him, or perhaps he indulged his children a few luxuries in the harsh conditions of Afghanistan.

CHARACTER AND PERSONALITY

If reconstructing the details of bin Laden's life presents serious challenges, then discerning the nature and development of his personality and character poses even more formidable problems. In most societies only the closest family members and a few trusted friends know a person across the majority of his/her life. In the tight extended family and kinship groups of Saudi Arabia, the number may be considerably larger, but family members are more reluctant to talk to outsiders about a relative. When the relative becomes notorious, cast out by family and country, their ranks close even tighter. The closed, secretive nature of the kingdom compounds the difficulty in gathering information as does as the majority Wahhabist sect's opposition to celebrating birthdays and taking photographs. What remains to be gleaned by the biographer are a relative handful of impressions, most from people interviewed after the man had grown to mythic proportions.

As a youth Osama bin Laden made little impression on those around him. Were it not for his unusual height, he might have attracted little attention. Friends and teachers remember him as being introverted and quiet, intelligent but not particularly invested in school work. One teacher described him as "more courteous than the average student."[29] His intense religious devotion seems to have developed after his father's death, but even that was not unusual for Saudi Arabia. Nothing known about his behavior during childhood and adolescence suggests that he would develop into a murderous fanatic. Far from being inherently violent, he seems to have avoided confrontation. When a friend pushed away a bully about to strike bin Laden, Osama stopped the friend from fighting. "I went running to the guy, and I pushed him away from Osama and solved [the] problem this way," Khalid Batarfi recalled. "But then Osama came to me, and said, 'You know, if you waited a few minutes, I would have solved the problem peacefully.' "[30]

Witnesses disagree on his leadership ability. Most accounts of his charismatic qualities come after he had become infamous in the West and revered in parts of the Muslim world. As an adolescent and a young man, he seems to have been deeply impressionable, perhaps seeking the father figure he had lost as a child. One of his closest friends described Osama as "a good soldier; send him anywhere and he will follow orders." However, the same friend also declared him to be "a natural leader," one who "leads by example and by hints more than direct orders."[31] However, Prince Bandar the former Saudi ambassador to the United States had a much lower opinion of Osama's leadership ability. "I thought he couldn't lead eight ducks across the street," Bandar declared.[32]

Bin Laden fell easily under the spell of strong personalities who could appeal to and perhaps manipulate his inherent piety. The Syrian physical education teacher in high school recruited him for his study group and launched him on the path to jihad. Mohammed Qutb inspired him with the teachings of his brother Sayyid. Abdullah Azzam persuaded him to go to Pakistan to help fund and organize the war against the Soviets in Afghanistan. There he fell under the sway of the fanatic Egyptian doctor Ayman al-Zawahiri. Azzam and Zawahiri competed for Osama as a prize to be won for his personal wealth and the money he could raise for their respective causes. They sometimes treated him as a valuable asset not as an equal.

HOBBIES AND INTERESTS

Bin Laden's aversion to most things secular left him few options for hobbies and pastimes. He did, however, develop a passion for raising and racing horses. He is also an accomplished rider. He raised horses on his

Saudi farm before leaving for the Afghan war against the Soviets. When he moved to Sudan, he attended races there, although he probably did not bet on the outcome. In the rugged terrain of Afghanistan, horses were essential part of the struggle, first against the Americans and then against the Soviets.

RADICAL IN SEARCH FOR A CAUSE

By the standards of Saudi Arabia and his social class, Osama bin Laden does not stand out. He was more religious than most of his contemporaries but within the bounds of a very conservative theocratic society. Although wealthy by any standard, he did not live the life of an international playboy pursued by his eldest half-brother Salem. Growing up he never wanted for anything, but neither did he live a life of luxury. He had the ability to earn a university degree but little interest in doing so. He preferred an active life to the classroom or a profession. Had circumstances been otherwise, he would probably have lived an unremarkable life of quiet piety as a very junior member of the vast bin Laden family given business responsibilities commensurate with his abilities, which seem to have been quite modest.

The historical circumstances in which bin Laden grew up were, however, exceptional. He came of age at a unique time of crisis and empowerment in the Muslim world. The six-day Arab-Israeli War of 1967 humiliated the Arab world and discredited secular pan-Arab nationalism. The Islamic revolution in Iran and the attack on Mecca's Grand Mosque, both occurring in 1979, demonstrated how much a small, but determined group of radicals could accomplish. The Soviet invasion of Afghanistan, also in 1979, gave devote Muslims a chance to wage a holy war in defense of an Islamic state attacked by godless communists. Osama saw in the Afghan war an opportunity to put his beliefs into practice. The conflict may also have appealed to his restlessness for activity and need for attention. In that crusade the man would graduate from radical to extremist; he would become a myth in both the West and the Islamic world.

NOTES

1. Details based upon *Saudi Arabia, A Brief History*, at http://www.mideastweb.org/arabiahistory.htm, accessed July 1, 2009.

2. Excerpt of official history of Saudi Binladin Group, available on the company website, http://www.sbgpbad.ae/default.asp?action=article&ID=20, accessed July 27, 2009.
3. Steve Coll, *The Bin Ladens: An Arabian Family in the American Century* (New York: Penguin, 2008) provides the best account of the family's rise to wealth and prominence.
4. Coll concludes that the marriage lasted a "relatively short time," although the details are not certain.
5. Ibid., p. 151.
6. Ibid., p. 107.
7. Interview with Jamal Ismail for al Al Jazeera television aired in 1999 in Yusef H. Aboul-Enein, "Osama bin-Laden interview, June 1999: entering the mind of an adversary," *Military Review*, September-October 2004, http://findarticles.com/p/articles/mi_m0PBZ/is_5_84/ai_n7069249/?tag=content;col1, accessed, July 27, 2009.
8. Account of Khaled Batarfi in Peter Bergen, *The Osama bin Laden I Know* (New York: Free Press, 2006), pp. 15, 240.
9. Steve Coll, *The Bin Ladens: An Arabian Family in the American Century* (New York: Penguin Press, 2008), p. 140. One source claims that attended another Lebanese boarding school prior to attending the Quaker one, but this is not confirmed.
10. Account of Christian Akerblad, former owner of Hotel Astoria in Falun, Sweden, in Bergen, *The Osama bin Laden I Know*, p. 11.
11. Coll, *The Bin Ladens,* p. 209.
12. Carmen bin Laden, *Inside the Kingdom* (2004), excerpted in ibid., pp. 20-21.
13. Osama bin Laden's mother Alia, quoted in ibid., p. 138.
14. Kahled Batarfi, quoted in ibid., p. 142.
15. Dan Korem, *Rage of the Random Actor* (Richardson, TX: International Focus Press, 2005), pp. 146-150, suggests that bin Laden fits his definition of a random actor prone to terrorist activity. Intriguing as the argument is, it is impossible to verify.
16. Christopher Browning, *Ordinary Men: Special Police Battalion 101 and the Final Solution in Poland.*
17. Coll, *The Bin Ladens*, p. 201.
18. Osama bin Laden's mother Alia, quoted in ibid., p. 139.
19. Recollection of Brian Fyfield-Shayler in Jason Burke, "The Making of the World's Most Wanted Man," *Observer,* 28 October 2001, http://www.guardian.co.uk/news/2001/oct/28/world.terrorism, accessed, July 28, 2009.
20. Coll, *The Bin Ladens.*
21. Ibid.

22. Account of Jamal Khalifa in ibid., p. 17.
23. Lawrence Wright, *The Looming Tower: Al-Qaeda and the Road to 9/11* (New York: Alfred Knopf, 2006), p. 193.
24. Ibid., pp. 80-82.
25. Ibid., pp. 252-3.
26. Ibid., p. 194.
27. Ibid., pp. 253-254.
28. Account of Yeslam bin Laden in ibid., p. 20.
29. Account of Brian Fyfield Shayler in ibid., p. 8.
30. Account of Khaled Batarfi in Henry Schuster, "Boyhood Friend Struggles with bin Laden Terror," CNN, August 21, 2006, available at http://www.rickross.com/reference/alqaeda/alqaeda77.html, accessed July 28, 2009.
31. Batarfi in Bergen, *The Osama bin Laden I Know*, pp. 13-14.
32. Korem, *Rage of the Random Actor*, p. 146.

CHAPTER 2

OSAMA'S WORLDVIEW

The complex beliefs, attitudes, and subconscious assumptions that make up a person's worldview develop over time. Formed from the prevailing norms of society and shaped by family and friends, worldviews may be further influenced by personal experience and world events. Depending on individual psychology, a person may modify his or her views later in life or become more convinced of their validity. In the case of Osama bin Laden events conspired to turn his religious piety into a dangerous fanaticism that grew more rigid as he aged.

SOCIAL AND HISTORICAL CONTEXT

Osama bin Laden did not begin life with a worldview. Like everyone else, he was born into a family and society with well established beliefs a prevailing system of norms, attitudes, and beliefs. These forces unconsciously shaped him as he grew up in the bin Laden family within the conservative kingdom of Saudi Arabia. When he entered school, teachers, mentors, and friends further molded his outlook as did the events he experienced directly through participating in them or vicariously through the media of print and television. As he matured, he also encountered conflicting ideas and examples of how to live. Like any young person, he had to reconcile these conflicts and integrate them into his own outlook and system of beliefs. Understanding Osama's worldview requires first examining the social and cultural context into which he was born and second, considering the people and events that shaped his thinking as he matured.

Osama bin Laden grew up during a period of rapid and at times traumatic transition in Saudi Arabia and the broader Middle East. The development of Saudi Arabia from medieval kingdom into modern state carried the bin Laden family from poverty to wealth. Mohammed bin Laden had started as a day laborer and gone on to found a successful construction firm, which his son Salem built into an international conglomerate. Osama grew up as the impact of oil wealth began to be felt throughout Saudi Arabia. He also witnessed some of the greatest shocks suffered by the Islamic world and took what he saw as their lessons to heart.

CRUCIAL EVENTS

Among these events none affected Osama bin Laden and his contemporaries the defeat of three Arab armies by Israel during the Six-Day War. In June 1967, Israel destroyed an Egyptian invasion force in a pre-emptive strike. During the ensuing week it defeated the armies of Jordan, Syria, and Iraq. The victory gave Israel control of the Sinai, Gaza, the West Bank, and the Golan Heights and created another wave of Palestinian refugees. The loss of East Jerusalem hit the Muslim world especially hard. East Jerusalem contained the ancient city of David and the holiest sites of Judaism and Christianity. It also contained the Mosque of Omar, popularly known as "the Dome of the Rock," the third holiest site in Islam. Perched atop the mount where Solomon's temple had once stood, the mosque enclosed a granite outcropping believed to be the point from which the Prophet Mohammed ascended to heaven during his famous night journey.

The Six-Day War was the third disastrous defeat suffered by Arab nations at the hands of Israel. The worst humiliation had come in 1948, when the newly created state defeated five Arab armies in its battle to survive. In 1956, the Israelis had triumphed with the help of France and Britain, although they had been forced to return the Sinai in what came to be known as the Suez Crisis. The Arabs would suffer yet another defeat in the 1973 Yom Kippur War. Conservative Muslims gave the defeats a theological interpretation. God had turned his back on Muslims who had abandoned the *suna* (example) of the Prophet to embrace Western ideas and values. Only by returning to the true path of Islam could Arab Muslims regain the prosperity and position of primacy in the Middle East they had once enjoyed.

The suffering of Palestinians, loss of the Dome of the Rock, and ultimately the very existence of Israel would become major tenets of Osama bin Laden's worldview. He would ultimately blame the United States for creating and supporting this "Zionist-Crusader" outpost in the Middle East. The relationship between the two countries has been more complicated than the general public in both countries or the Arab world realize. While the U.S. had pressured Britain to allow more Jewish refugees into what had then been the Mandate of Palestine and been among the first to recognize the new state, it had given Israel little support during the next two decades. Only in the aftermath of the Six-Day War had the relationship between the two countries become close. The U.S. provided crucial support in the form of military equipment and supplies during the Yom Kippur War. American foreign policy has tried to steer a tortuous course between the twin pillars of its Middle East policy: desire to placate Arab states who supply most of the Western world's oil and historic friendship to Israel. The presence of a strong Zionist lobby, which now consists of both members of the American Jewish community and conservative Christians, who consider Jewish control of Israel a prelude to Christ's second coming, encourages bin Laden's belief in Jewish conspiracies.

When his worldview had matured, bin Laden explained what he saw as the relationship between Israel and the U.S. "The leaders in America and in other countries as well have fallen victim to Jewish Zionist blackmail," he told an interviewer. "They have mobilized their people against Islam and against Muslims."[1] After 9/11, bin Laden explained that the Palestinian cause had in part motivated the devastating attack. "We swore that America wouldn't live in security until we live it truly in Palestine," he proclaimed.[2] Like many Islamist extremists, Osama saw a broader Jewish-American conspiracy at work in the Middle East. "What is happening in Palestine is merely a model that the

Zionist-American alliance wishes to impose upon the rest of the region," he declared: "the killing of men, women and children, prisons, terrorism, the demolition of homes, the razing of farms, the destruction of factories." Their ultimate goal, he warned, was to create a "greater Israel" in the Middle East.[3]

A series of events in 1979 profoundly shaped Osama bin Laden's worldview and launched him on the path of global jihad. In January of that year, Ayatollah Ruhollah Musavi Khomeni led a revolution that overthrew the Shah of Iran and replaced his government with an Islamic Republic. The Iranian Revolution provided a powerful example for groups committed to an Islamic revival throughout the Muslim world. In November Islamist radicals seized the Grand Mosque in Mecca, site of the Ka'ba, Islam's holiest shrine and proclaimed their leader the Mahdi, the Muslim redeemer prophesied to come in the Islamic year 1400 (1979). Saudi and French special forces recaptured the Mosque in a bloody twelve-day siege. Because violence within the shrine is strictly forbidden, the Saudi government secured a fatwa (religious ruling or proclamation) from the country's leading cleric justifying the counter-terrorism operation.

While it is not clear how this event affected twenty-one year old Osama, the siege of the Grand Mosque challenged the monarchy's theological legitimacy, a theme he would take up later in life.[4] Years later he criticized King Fahd's handling of the incident. Bin Laden would later claim that King Fahd had "defiled" the Grand Mosque in the way that he conducted the assault to recapture it. "He showed stubbornness, acted against the advice of everyone, and sent tracked and armored vehicles into the mosque."[5] This comment offered in hindsight may be the result of bin Laden's later break with the monarchy, or it may genuinely indicate that the siege of the Grand Mosque began his disillusionment with the house of Saud.

The third major event of the epic year 1979 would prove to be the most critical. In December 1979, Soviet forces entered the central Asian country of Afghanistan to prop up its communist puppet government. The invasion began a ten year war between the Soviets and Afghan insurgents covertly supported by the U.S. and Saudi Arabia. The conflict would draw in foreign *mujahedeen* (holy warriors) from the many Muslim countries, especially those in the Arab world. Among these would fighters would be Osama bin Laden.

TRADITIONAL ISLAM

Contrary to popular belief, Islam no more promotes violence than does any other world religion. Like many other faiths, however, it has been perverted by a minority of practitioners to promote their extremist agenda. The high profile of these extremists in the western media has encouraged the unfortunate belief that they speak for the majority of Muslims. Clarification of the religion's core beliefs must, therefore, precede discussion of how Osama bin Laden and his followers have appropriated and misused them.

Islam is the last of three great monotheisms tracing its origins to the patriarch Abraham. While Jews trace their lineage from Abraham through his son Isaac, Muslims claim descent from Abraham's son Ishmael. According to Islamic teaching, the Archangel Gabriel appeared to the Prophet Muhammad while he was fasting and praying in a cave outside of Mecca during the "night of power" in 610 C.E. Over the next several years the Archangel revealed divine truth to the Prophet. Written down shortly after the Mohammed's death, these revelations became the *Holy Quran*, the sacred text of Islam. Gabriel proclaimed that God (*Allah* in Arabic) had spoken the same message twice before, first to the Jews through Moses, and then to the Christians through Jesus of Nazareth. Because the followers of these prophets had corrupted the revelation, God decided to give humanity one last chance, speaking truth through Gabriel to Mohammed, the last or "seal" of the prophets. Because God's revelation came to Mohammed in Arabic, the *Quran* cannot be translated. Muslims learn Arabic to read the original text and devout believers try to memorize the entire book. Illiterate Muslims may memorize important verses learned orally.

The core teaching of the *Quran* consist in what Muslims refer to as the "five pillars of Islam." Each pillar expresses a key doctrine of the faith. *Shahadah*, the first pillar, requires the believer to proclaim the oneness of God and submit to the divine will. "Islam" literally means "submission to the will of God," and a "Muslim" is "one who submits." Like Judaism, Islam rejects the Christian trinity, teaching that God is one, whole, and indivisible. Muslims revere Jesus as a great prophet, mentioned more frequently in the *Quran* than Mohammed, but reject the belief that he is God incarnate, born of a virgin and raised from the dead. Like

Christianity, Islam seeks converts. *Tawhid* requires Muslims to proclaim the core truth of their faith: "There is no God but Allah, and Mohammed is his prophet." By speaking this declaration of faith (*Shahda)* three times in front of witnesses, one becomes a Muslim.

Salat, the second pillar of Islam, requires Muslims to pray five times a day facing Mecca. The first prayer takes place before dawn, the second around noon, the third at dusk, the fourth just after sunset, and the fifth before retiring for the night. Prayers must be performed prostrate in a clean place free of blood and excrement. They usually take about five minutes to complete. Prayers may be rescheduled or made up as necessity dictates. A Muslim surgeon does not stop an operation to perform Salat. On Friday (*Jama*) Muslims perform the mid-day prayer at their Mosque, if their circumstances permit. Jama Salat includes a homily or short sermon by the Imam (Muslim cleric) or a member of the congregation. Those who consider Muslims overly devout because of their need to pray five times a day would do well to remember that Christianity commands its followers to "pray without ceasing."[6] Traditional Judaism prescribes prayers for virtually every daily activity.

Zakat, the giving of alms, constitutes the third pillar of Islam. The *Quran* requires Muslims to give 2.5% of their annual worth to charity. Once a formal tax that funded government activities beyond poor relief, *Zakat* has become an ideal towards which devote Muslims strive. Just as Jews and Christians consider the Biblical tithe (one tenth of annual income) a desirable goal, even if they fall short of meeting it, Muslims living in secular states often aim to donate to their Mosque and/or Islamic charities as close to the specified amount as they can afford.

Sawm (fasting), the fourth pillar of Islam, requires Muslims to fast during *Ramadan*, the ninth month of the Muslim lunar calendar, the month during which Mohammed received his revelation from the Archangel Gabriel. During Ramadan Muslims consume no food or drink (including water) from sunup to sundown and abstain from sex during daylight hours. Because the lunar calendar does not align accurately with the solar calendar in use to day, Ramadan occurs at a different time each year. When it falls during the summer, fasting for the long hours of daylight can be challenging. However, Islam approaches *Sawm* with the same grace and flexibility it applies to Salat. Pregnant women and men doing hard physical labor are not expected to fast, but they are encouraged to make up the fasting when they are physically able to do so.

Hajj, pilbrimage, is the fifth pillar of Islam. Every Muslim with the financial means to do so must make a pilgrimage to the holy city of Mecca once in his or her lifetime. Mecca's Grand Mosque contains an ancient shrine known as the *Ka'ba* (cube), placed there (according to tradition) by Abraham. By the time of the Prophet the *Ka'ba* had become the focus of polytheistic worship, which he condemned as idolatry. Gabriel called upon Mohammed to cleanse the *Ka'ba'* of the idols placed there by diverse worshipers. This cleansing mission set him on a collision course with the powerful tribes that controlled the caravan trade through Mecca. These groups profited from the religious activities at the *Ka'ba* in the same way shop owners and inn keepers in a medieval cathedral town benefited from veneration of the cathedral's relics. Pilgrims need food, a place to sleep, and other goods and services that they must purchase locally. Mohammed and his followers fled persecution in Mecca for the safety of neighboring Medina. There he raised an army, defeated an invading army in the famous Battle of the Trenches, and after a long struggle returned to Mecca in 632. He finally fulfilled the mission given him by the Archangel Gabriel twenty years before to purify the Ka'ba. *Hajj* commemorates the Prophet's journey from Medina to Mecca. Muslims who have made the pilgrimage add the term *Haji* (men) or *Hajia* (women) to their names, signifying that they have fulfilled this sacred duty.

Beyond the five pillars, Islam has an extensive system of beliefs and practices governing all aspects of life. As with any religion, observance varies widely and has been shaped by local culture. Muslims believe in a final judgment in which Allah welcomes the faithful into paradise and condemns the wicked to hell. They do not consume alcohol or narcotics in part because consuming these mind-altering drugs lowers inhibitions and can lead to a host of other sins. Islam has a dietary code very similar to Jewish Kosher laws. It prohibits consumption of blood, carrion (animals that have died spontaneously), pork, and any food sacrificed to idols. Like all religious leaders, the Prophet Mohammed provided a host of rulings affecting all areas of personnel and social life. Known as the *Hadiths* or "sayings" of the prophet, these statements stand second only to the *Holy*

Quran in guiding Muslim behavior.[7] The *Quran,* the *Hadiths,* and the body of rulings by the *ulema* (religious scholars) form the basis of *sharia* (Islamic law) governing Muslim states such as Oman, Saudi Arabia, and Pakistan. Sharia varies from country to country and has been influenced by other legal traditions. The extreme, inflexible version of *sharia* enforced by the Taliban in Afghanistan is neither typical nor endorsed by the majority of Muslim legal scholars.

Like any body of sacred literature, the *Quran* and the *Hadiths* have had to be interpreted, especially as new issues, unforeseen by the Prophet arose over the centuries. The dress code adopted by Muslims illustrates the complexity of Muslim belief and practice. The Prophet instructed women to cover all parts of their bodies except their faces and hands. Muslim women who embrace secularism may consider this dress code as a manifestation of medieval Arabic culture no longer applicable today. In much of the West and in most Muslim countries, women cover their hair with the traditional head scarf known as an *hijab.* In more conservative societies, women will add a veil covering their mouth and nose. Only extremely conservative groups like the Taliban require that women be covered from head to toe in the cumbersome burqa.

Like their Jewish and Christian counterparts, Muslim scholars have had to rule on a host of issues neither expressly forbidden nor explicitly allowed by the *Quran* and *Hadiths.* For example, coffee became available in the Arabian Peninsula long after the Prophet's death. Was the new drink *haram* (forbidden) or *halal* (permitted)? Reasoning by analogy, the ulema concluded that since coffee had none of the undesirable effects of alcohol, believers could drink it. The Apostle Paul faced similar challenges when asked to mediate disputes in the early Christian church. "Is it permissible to eat food sacrificed to idles," the Corinthian Church asked. "Yes," Paul replied, "unless doing so causes potential converts to turn away from Christianity."[8]

SUNNI AND SHI'A

Soon after the Mohammed's death a dispute arose that would eventually divide the Muslim world into two broad groups. Like all leaders of his time, the Prophet Mohammed had both religious and political authority.

His contemporaries could not even have imagined separating the two, let alone effecting the separation. When Mohammed died, his followers argued over who should succeed him. The majority believed that the keeper of the prophet's *Sunnah* (traditions) should be chosen from among his followers by the principal of *shura* (consultation). This group became known as "Sunnis." Mohammed's cousin and son-in-law Ali disagreed, arguing that the *Caliph* (guardian) should be a member of the prophet's own family. He claimed the title for himself and his line as Prophet's most direct male heir. Those who supported this interpretation of Mohammed's wishes called themselves "partisans of Ali," "*Shi'a*" in Arabic. Ali became the fourth Caliph in 658, but he ruled only until 661 when a rebel soldier assassinated him. Sunnis regained and maintained control of the Caliphate, which passed from Arab to Ottoman Turkish control in the Middle Ages and disappeared in 1924 when Mustapha Kemal established the modern secular state of Turkey. Most Shiites have historically followed the teachings of 12 Imams beginning with Ali himself and ending with Muhammad Ali Mahdi. Born in 868, Ali Mahdi disappeared from human view in 874. Prophesy holds that he will return to complete his work of making Islam the global religion at some future date.[9]

Other doctrinal differences divide Sunni and Shi'a Islam. Shi'a clergy typically play a greater role in religious life and politics than do Sunni Imams. This difference explains why clerics like Grand Ayatollah Sayyid Ali Husaini Sistani and Grand Ayatollah Mohammad Mohammad Sadeq al-Sadr enjoy such power and influence in contemporary Iraq. Like most Islamist extremists bin Laden came to consider Shi'a "*Kafirs*" (non-believers). Today 85-90% of Muslims are Sunni.

JIHAD

No Islamic concept has been so misunderstood as *jihad*, which is usually (and inaccurately) translated as "holy war." The Arabic noun *Jihad* derives from the verb *jhd*, which means "to strive or exert oneself." "Holy struggle" or "struggle for righteousness" thus more closely captures the meaning of the Arabic word *jihad* than does "holy war." Like Judaism and Christianity, Islam values all human life. "Take not life, which Allah hath made sacred, except by way of justice and law," the *Quran* instructs.[10]

Islam also requires Muslims to seek converts, and the so-called "sword verses" in the *Quran* do sanction violence against non-believers. However, like similar verses in the *Hebrew Bible* and the *New Testament*, these verses should not be taken out of context. The Prophet taught that *jihad* should be waged only in defense of Islam, and that warfare must be conducted according to rules distinguishing combatants from non-combatants and requiring humane treatment of captives. "Fight in the cause of Allah those who fight you, but do not transgress limits; for Allah loveth not transgressors," he instructed.[11] Mohammed called this defensive warfare "the lesser *jihad*." He then introduced the "greater *jihad*:"

> the struggle each Muslim undertakes to live a devout life in submission to the will of Allah.[12] "And strive in His cause as ye ought to strive, (with sincerity and under discipline)," the *Quran* proclaims. Allah "has chosen you, and has imposed no difficulties on you in religion; it is the cult of your father Abraham. It is He Who has named you Muslims, both before and in this (Revelation); that the Messenger may be a witness for you, and ye be witnesses for mankind! So establish regular Prayer, give regular Charity, and hold fast to Allah."[13]

SALAFISM AND WAHABISM

Like Christianity and Judaism, Islam has experience revival movements throughout its long history. Two of these movements, Salafism and Wahabism have shaped Saudi society and influenced the thinking of Osama bin Laden. The *Salafist* movement originated in the ninth century C.E., but the fourteenth-century Islamic scholar, Taqi al-Din Ahmad Ibn Taymiyya developed it more fully. Derived from the Arabic word *salaf* meaning "devout ancestor" (in reference to contemporaries of the Prophet Mohammed), *Salafism* calls upon Muslims to return to the pure teachings of the first *uma* (community of believers) to which the Prophet Mohammed belonged. In his call for revival Taymiyya rejected the orthodox Sunni Muslim teaching that forbids rebellion against Muslim rulers and allowed jihad against leaders who did not live and govern according to *sharia.*[14] "Since lawful warfare is essentially jihad and since its aim is that the religion is Allah's entirely [2:189, 8:39] and Allah's word is uppermost [9:40], therefore, according to all Muslims, *those who stand in the way of this aim must be fought*," Taymiyya proclaimed.[15] Those who must be fought thus included unjust Muslim rulers as well as non-Muslims.

In the 18th century a new Salafist revival occurred in Arabia. Like Taymiyya, Muhammad Ibn Abd al-Wahhab (1703-1792) called for a return to the purity of early Islam. The modern Saudi monarchy developed out of a 1745 alliance between al-Wahhab and the house of Saud, a partnership revived in 1932 by Abdul Aziz when he founded modern Saudi Arabia. In return for a guarantee that the kingdom would be governed by sharia, al-Wahhab and his descendants agreed to support the monarchy.[16] During the nineteenth century *Salafism* revived once more and spread to Egypt, Persia (Iran), and Syria, perhaps as a response to European colonialism.[17] In twentieth-century Egyptian Salafism would mutate into the deadly variant embraced by Osama bin Laden.

The problem with Salafism (or any other religious revival) is that its proponents claim that they alone know what purity of practice and belief truly is. They do not recognize and cannot accept that what they offer is an interpretation not infallible truth. Historians know very little about the Prophet Mohammed's Arabia. Any Salafist calls to return to that pristine age must, therefore be based more on conviction than historical evidence. Because revivalists cannot accept such relativism, they are usually among the most intolerant of believers.

THE MUSLIM BROTHERHOOD

Contemporary Salafism has its roots in Egypt, where a new movement known as "Islamism" began in the period between the two World Wars. In 1928, Hasan al-Banna established in Cairo an organization known as the Muslim Brotherhood. Like Ibn Taymiyya and al-Wahhab before him, al-Banna wished for a return to the world of the seventh century during which Islamic teaching governed all aspects of Muslim life. The impending end of colonialism, however, gave al-Banna's movement a new urgency as he saw a real opportunity regenerate Egyptian society. Competing for power after the British left would be the corrupt regime of King Farouk, widely seen as a British puppet, and later the secular and socialist Arab nationalism of Colonel Gamal Abdul Nasser. Al-Banna rejected both alternatives, arguing vehemently that the way to the future lay through the past. Only by rejecting the ways of the West and embracing their Islamic heritage could Egypt prosper. Al-Banna also elevated the lesser *jihad* above the greater and proclaimed it a Muslim duty more sacred than *Hajj.* "Many Muslims today mistakenly believe that fighting the enemy is *jihad asghar* (a lesser jihad) and that fighting one's ego is *jihad akbar* (a greater jihad)." This idea was mistaken, he declared.[18] Like Wahab, he believed that in addition to fighting non-believers, Muslims might also wage *jihad* against tyrannical Muslim rulers.

The Egyptian government shut down the Brotherhood's offices and organs in 1948 and assassinated al-Banna in 1949, in retaliation for the assassination of the Egyptian prime minister. The Brotherhood, of course, continued to operate and even grow, albeit clandestinely. A new spokesman for the movement emerged after al-Banna's death, developed his ideas further, and spread them farther abroad. Sayid Qutb joined the Muslim Brotherhood in the early 1950s and became its most famous spokesman. "Islam, then, is the only Divine way of life which brings out the noblest human characteristics, developing and using them for the construction of human society," he proclaimed. "Islam has remained unique in this respect to this day. Those who deviate from this system and want some other system, whether it be based on nationalism, color and race, class struggle, or similar corrupt theories, are truly enemies of mankind!"[19] In addition to declaring western nationalism and socialism inappropriate for Muslim societies, Qutb rejected the idea that *jihad* was purely defensive warfare. "Thus, wherever an Islamic community exists which is a concrete example of the Divinely-ordained system of life," he asserted, "it has a God-given right to step forward and take control of the political authority so that it may establish the Divine system on earth, while it leaves the matter of belief to individual conscience."[20] Although Qutb and the Brotherhood cooperated with a military coup led by Colonel Gamal Abdul Nasser to overthrow King Farouk in 1952, the movement turned against Nasser when he refused to create the hoped-for Islamic republic. Nasser believed Egypt's future lay in embracing western secularism, nationalism, and socialism, all of which were anathema to Qutb.

Like al-Banna before him, Qutb died a martyr's death. Nasser executed him in 1967 for plotting against the government. His martyrdom helped the movement grow. During his years of imprisonment, Qutb wrote

Milestones, a detailed articulation his Islamist worldview specifically rebutting the political philosophy of Egypt's secular government. Osama bin Laden read this book as a student and was profoundly influenced by it. Following Qutb's death the Muslim Brotherhood split into factions. While the Brotherhood pursued its goals through education and the political process, Islamic Jihad embraced violence. Its eventual leader Dr. Ayman al-Zawahiri would help to convert bin Laden to the cause of global jihad.

Qutb's writings and the example of his life profoundly influenced young Osama. His friend at University, Jamal Khalifa, described this influence. For his parents' generation, Khalifa explained, Islam was a tradition that structured their lives. Qutb, however, "was concentrating on the meaning of Islam that it's the way of life." According to Khalifa, Qutb "influenced every Muslim in that period of time." He also noted that Qutb's brother Mohammed, a visiting professor at King Abdul Aziz University during the late 1970s, used to give lectures which Khalifa and bin Laden attended. "He was giving us very good lessons about education—how to educate our children.[21]

Because modern Islamism offers an alternative form of governance to the secularism of Nasser and other Arab nationalists, it is sometimes called political Islam. The European Enlightenment of the eighteenth century introduced the idea that church and state should separate. This concept enshrined in the U.S. Constitution made religion a purely private matter. Individuals could worship as they pleased within a civil society governed by non-religious law. Islamism (political Islam) rejects this notion, insisting that Islam govern all areas of life from morality to diet and dress. Because this desire for a theocratic state in which religion governs all aspects of life harkens back to a what in the West is a pre-enlightenment world, Western observers often mistakenly view Islamism as an atavistic movement rather than as contemporary effort to find a purely Muslim solution to the challenges of modernity.

THE ISLAMIC AWAKENING

Islamism made little headway outside Egypt and, even there, remained marginalized. Saudi Arabia alone welcomed Muslim Brotherhood members fleeing persecution. The Brotherhood's Salafist views accorded well with the Kingdom's conservative, Wahhabi Islam, although Saudi clerics did not support violent jihad. In addition, the Saudi monarchy saw Nasser's pan-Arabism as a threat to its existence and considered the Muslim Brotherhood a useful counter to Nasser's popularity in the Arab world.[22] For most educated Arabs, however, emulating the West seemed to offer the best way forward.

This view suffered a severe shock in June 1967. Within six days the army and air force of Israel soundly defeated the forces of Egypt, Syria, Iraq, and Jordan. They captured the Old City of Jerusalem with its Wailing Wall and Dome of the Rock, the West Bank of the Jordan River, the Golan Heights, and the Sinai Peninsula. This humiliating loss led many Arabs to question the secular basis of their governments. Those of a religious bent wondered if God were not punishing them for embracing Western decadence. Amid this turmoil, Islamism grew more popular. Many Muslims now believed that the way to the future lay through the past. Only by returning to the values and social system of the prophet's *uma* (community of believers) could Muslim civilization recover the stature it had once known under the medieval caliphs. This Islamist revival became known as the "awakening."

Most Islamists do not, however, use or condone violence to achieve their goals. Islamism today is a broad movement sometimes called the "New Islamic Discourse." Muslim scholars, religious leaders, and intellectuals within this movement do not wish to turn the clock back to the seventh century. Instead they seek to embrace the technological and material advantages of modernity while preserving Islamic faith, traditions, and culture. The movement does not reject modernity, but it does challenge the notion that the only way to modernize is by emulating the example of the West. Many scholars in the movement accept the advantages of science and technology but still wish to live in religiously based societies governed by the principal of consultation rather than mass democracy. They accept the complementarity but not the strict equality of the sexes. They wish to decide how best to order their own affairs and bitterly resent the U.S. or any other nation seeking to impose its way of life upon them.[23] Although many Islamists blame U.S. foreign policy for threatening their way of life, the real challenge comes from the forces of globalization, which no one really controls.

FAMILY

In addition to the intellectual currents of the era, the elaborate bin Laden family system influenced Osama's outlook. His mother remarried within a few years of his birth, and his father died when Osama was only nine. Although he revered his father, Osama could have had little contact with a man whose numerous wives and construction projects kept him on the move. Mohammed's simple lifestyle and piety influenced his young son, but as Osama grew to manhood, he also had the countervailing example of his eldest half brother Salem. Salem, who became patriarch of the family upon his father's death in 1967, lived the life of an international playboy. He took Osama on some of his trips abroad, although his younger brother does not seem to have succumbed to the temptations of the flesh Salem enjoyed in Europe and America.[24] For a complex variety of personal reasons Osama practiced the conservative Wahabi Islam devoutly and consistently.

Those who knew bin Laden as a young man attest to his desire to emulate his father's work ethic and simple life. Khaled Batarfi described how Osama differed from his brothers in this respect. "That's the way the bin Ladins are. They study and work all of them, all the people I know," Batarfi observed, "but he [Osama] was different because he used to work with his hands, go drive tractors and like his father eat with the workers, work from dawn to sundown, tirelessly in the field. So he wasn't the rich boy."[25]

OSAMA'S EMERGING WORLDVIEW

How precisely the complex mix of intellectual currents, contemporary events, and family circumstances shaped Osama's worldview remains unclear. While the core tenets of his conservative Muslim faith were established by the time he left high school, his political views had only begun to take shape. The writings of Qutb, the teachings of his mentor Abdullah Azzam, and the radial views of Islamic Jihad would complete the formation of his worldview.

A Saudi journalist who knew bin Laden when he lived in Jeddah provided what may be the most succinct and incisive assessment of his beliefs before the life-changing experience of Afghanistan. "Osama was just like many of us who become part of the [Muslim] Brotherhood movement in Saudi Arabia. The only difference which set him apart from me and others, he was more religious," Jamal Khashoggi recalled.

> He adhered to a very strict interpretation of Islam. He did not smoke, refused to shake hands with women, and watched only the news on television. No pictures adorned the walls of his home as he considered art un-Islamic. Although he belonged to a wealthy family he insisted on living a simple life, eschewing all extravagance.[26]

Osama bin Laden's emerging worldview has been dubbed "jihadist salafism." It consists of the core beliefs of the larger Islamist movement: a rejection of Western law, political systems, and especially secularism as inappropriate for Muslim societies. Osama also came to believe that jihad was a duty, what Islamist extremists call the "sixth pillar of Islam." His jihad would be waged aggressively against Islam's enemies, near and far. He would eventually be persuaded that violence could be used against other Muslims, especially rulers who failed to govern according to Sharia. However, he had not yet fully embraced these radical beliefs before he left Saudi Arabia. The Afghan war against the Soviets would be the next step in his journey towards terrorism.

NOTES

1. Osama bin Laden, May 1998 in Raymond Ibrahim, ed. and trans., *The Al-Qaeda Reader* (New York: Broadway Books, 3007), p. 275.
2. Osama bin Laden in ibid., p. 276.
3. Osama bin Laden in ibid., p. 277.
4. Steve Coll, *The Bin Ladens: An Arabian Family in the American Century* (New York: Penguin, 2008), pp. 228-229.
5. Michael Young, "Al-Qaeda's Forerunner: An interview with author and journalist Yaroslav Trofimov, on his latest book bin Laden, describing the 1979 takeover of the Grand Mosque in Mecca," *Reason Online*, September 27, 2007, available at http://www.reason.com/news/printer/122686.html, accessed July 28, 2009.
6. *New Oxford Annotated Bible* (New York: Oxford University Press, 1991), *New Testament,* 1 Thessalonians, 5:17, p. 295.
7. For a more detailed discussion of Muslim beliefs and practices see Frederick Mathewson Denny, *An Introduction to Islam*, second edition (New York: Macmillan, 1994; 1st ed., 1985).

8. *New Oxford Annotated Bible, New Testament,* I Corinthians, 8:1-11, pp. 237-8.
9. Denny, *An Introduction to Islam,* pp. 211-14.
10. Holy Quran, Sura 6:151, English translation available at, http://www.islamicity.com/mosque/QURAN/6.htm#151.
11. Holy Quran, Sura, 2:190, available at http://www.islamicity.com/mosque/QURAN/2.htm#191
12. Explanation of Jihad is based on, Seyyed Hossein Nasr, Prof. of Islamic Studies, George Washington U., "Spiritual Significance of Jihad," http://www.islamicity.com/articles/Articles.asp?ref=IC0407-2391
13. Holy Quran, Sura 22:78, English translation available at, http://www.islamicity.com/mosque/QURAN/22.htm#78
14. Bernard Haykel, "Radical Salafism: Osama's Ideology," 2001, http://muslim-canada.org/binladendawn.html#copyrightauthor The author teaches Islamic Law at New York University.
15. Ahmad ibn Taymiyyah, *The Religious and Moral Doctrine of Jihad,* translated and excerpted at http://www.islamistwatch.org/main.html
16. Ibid., p. 51.
17. Giles Kepel, *Jihad: In Search of Political Islam* translated by Anthony F. Roberts (Cambridge, MA: The Belknap Press of Harvard University Press, 2002), p. 220.
18. Hasan al-Banna, *Jihad,* translated and available at http://www.islamistwatch.org/main.html.
19. Sayd Qutb, *Milestones,* originally published in 1964; translated and available at http://www.islamistwatch.org/texts/qutb/Milestones/characteristics.html
20. Sayd Qutb, http://www.islamistwatch.org/texts/qutb/Milestones/jihad.html.
21. Jamal Khalifa in Peter Bergen, *The Osama bin Laden I Knew,* p. 19.
22. Coll, *The Bin Ladens,* p. 203.
23. Sherifa Zuhur, *A Hundred Osamas: Islamist Threats and the Future of Counterinsurgency,* (Carlisle Barracks, PA: Strategic Studies Institute, 2005), pp. 19-23.
24. Zuhur provides the best account of the bin Laden family.
25. Khalid Batarfi, in Bergen, *Osama bin Laden I Knew,* p. 22.
26. Jamal Khashoggi in ibid., p. 21.

Chapter 3

AFGHANISTAN

Events conspired to catapult Osama bin Laden from relative obscurity to the center of world politics in under a decade. The epic year was 1979. As already noted, the Iranian Revolution and the siege of the Grand Mosque sent tremors throughout the Muslim world. At the time, Bin Laden had little to say about either incident, although he later criticized Saudi authorities for using excessive force to retake the Golden Mosque. He may have been inspired by these events nonetheless, for he soon took up the cause of violent jihad in a very direct and personal way.

AFGHAN WAR

It would be difficult to exaggerate the impact of the Afghan War against the Soviets on Osama bin Laden. For the first time in his life he traveled far from home and remained abroad for several years. On April 14, 1979, Soviet forces entered Afghanistan to back its tottering communist regime against a growing Islamist insurgency. The Soviets built up their forces throughout the year and, on December 27, overthrew the president and commenced an offensive against the insurgents. Their force strength eventually numbered more than 100,000 troops operating in support of an Afghan army of roughly the same size. With little experience of counterinsurgency and less patience for waging it, the Soviets conducted a brutal campaign against the general population, whom they believed to be harboring and supporting the insurgents. An estimated one million Afghans died in the fighting.[1] Eighty per cent of those killed were civilians.[2] Tens of thousands more fled to refugee camps across the border in neighboring Pakistan.

Although heavily outgunned by the Soviets, the insurgents had definite advantages and some powerful friends. They operated amid a sympathetic population in ideal guerrilla terrain, which they knew intimately. Anxious to offset Iranian influence in the region, Saudi Arabia funneled money to the Afghan insurgents. The U.S. also saw an opportunity to hurt the Soviets in the same way the Soviets had hurt the U.S. in Vietnam. Supplying the enemy of your enemy was a cherished Cold War tactic. The conflict thus became a proxy war in which the Americans fought the Russians via the Afghans. National Security Advisor Zbigniew Brzezinski sent an almost gleeful memo to President Jimmy Carter on the very day Soviet forces crossed the border. "We now have the opportunity of giving to the USSR its Vietnam War," he wrote. "Indeed, for almost 10 years, Moscow had to carry on a war unsupportable by the government, a conflict that brought about the demoralization and finally the breakup of the Soviet empire."[3] The insurgents received cash and weapons, including highly effective surface-to-air missiles capable of shooting down the lethal MI-24 "Hind" helicopter gunship.

To avoid a direct confrontation with the Soviets, the CIA had to funnel aid to the insurgents through a third party. Fortunately, the government of Pakistan was more than willing to help. Embroiled in a perennial conflict with India over Kashmir, Pakistan needed to secure its western border in order to concentrate on its eastern one. Because this policy of "strategic depth" necessitated a friendly government in Afghanistan, Pakistan eagerly supported the Islamist insurgency against the Soviets. The Pakistanis calculate quite accurately that an Islamist government in Kabul would be unable to cooperate with Hindu "infidels" in New Delhi. Pakistan's Inter-Services Intelligence Bureau (ISI) distributed U.S. and Saudi funds to the various insurgent groups.

ENTER THE MUJIHADEEN

The Afghan insurgents not only garnered covert support from the U.S. and Saudi Arabia, they also attracted volunteers from all over the Muslim world. Inspired by Islamist teaching these foreign *mujahedeen* (holy warriors) flocked to Afghanistan to wage jihad against the Godless Communists in defence of an Islamic state. The commitment and quality of these volunteers varied widely. Some had the willingness to fight but lacked the training to be effective soldiers. Others, particularly sons of wealthy Saudis, engaged in a perverse form of disaster tourism, showing up for a few weeks during school vacations to play at being guerrillas. Insurgent commanders tolerated these young men because of the resources they and/or their countries provided. Foreign fighters never numbered more than a few thousand at any one time and had no appreciable impact on the outcome of the war.[4] One Saudi journalist succinctly described the movement. "Altogether, people who spent six years and people who spent six days, maybe the number will come up to ten thousand," he wrote. "Because there was even jihad tour. Jihad vacation."[5] His count totalled all those who spent time in Afghanistan during a ten year period. The number of fighters available at any one time was a fraction of that number, those with ability and training, even fewer. However, in the folk mythology of al-Qaeda the role of the mujahedeen grew to epic proportions, empowering the movement to believe that it could accomplish anything.

SERVICE BUREAU

As a young man of 21, Osama bin Laden did not immediately race to Afghanistan to join the fight. He had not yet even embraced any form of political Islam. He did, however, fall under the influence of Abdullah Azzam, a Palestinian Islamist deeply committed to radical Islamism. Azzam and Osama held many beliefs in common. Azzam belonged to the Muslim Brotherhood, and bin Laden had read with enthusiasm the works of Sayd Qutb, one of its leading lights. Azzam had been engaged in the Palestinian struggle since the 1960s, but the expulsion of the Palestine Liberation Organization from Jordan in 1971 temporarily stymied that effort. Osama had already developed empathy for the Palestinian cause and a deep visceral hatred of Israel. When the Soviets invaded Afghanistan, Azzam readily embraced the cause of the Afghan insurgents, even though he believed that Palestine was "the foremost Islamic problem." "Whoever can, from among the Arabs, fight jihad in Palestine, then he must start there," he instructed. "And, if he is not capable, then he must set out for Afghanistan. For the rest of the Muslims, I believe they should start their jihad in Afghanistan." The urgency and chances for success combined with the purity of the mujahedeen cause commended the struggle against the Soviets as a precursor to the fight against the Israelis.[6] As a visiting lecturer at King Abdul Aziz University in Jeddah in 1981, Azzam publicized the Afghan cause, no doubt with the approval of the Saudi government who also supported the mujahedeen. A Pakistani engineering student described Azzam's role in promoting the Afghan cause. "He used to be popular among Arab religious scholars, especially to Members of the Muslim Brotherhood," Jamal Ismail recalled. "He was the one who introduced the Afghan issue to all Muslims."[7]

Azzam visited bin Laden's home in Jeddah during the mid 1980s. Osama's university friend described the visit. "Osama invited me to his house in al Aziziyah [in Jeddah]," Jamal Khalifa recalled. "He has a building there, he was twenty-five, twenty-six, he's already married a couple of times. He told me Abdullah Azzam [was coming]. I knew Abdullah Azzam from his books. He's a very good writer and he's real educated so I was really eager to hear him when he started to talk about Afghanistan."[8] The references to bin Laden's age put the meeting date in 1983 or 1984.

No record of bin Laden's conversations with Azzam exist, but it is easy to conjecture from Azzam's writing and bin Laden's decision to relocate to Pakistan in order to aid the jihad. He sought to raise both money and recruits for the Afghan cause. While he understood the importance of resources, he rejected the notion that sending money to help the Afghan insurgents sufficed. "There is no doubt that jihad by one's person is superior to jihad by one's wealth," he argued. "Consequently, the rich in the time of the Prophet (saw), were not excused from participating with their persons, such as Uthman and Abdur Rahman Ibn Auf (ra). Because, the purification of the soul and the evolution of the spirit, is lifted to great heights in the midst of the battle."[9]

Azzam proclaimed jihad a sacred obligation incumbent upon Islamic communities and individual Muslims. "When a span of Muslim land is occupied jihad becomes individually obligatory (fard 'ayn) on the inhabitants of that piece of land," he proclaimed. This duty took precedence over all other obligations. "The woman may go out without her husband's permission with a mahram[relative], the one in debt without the permission of the one to whom he owes, the child without his father's permission." Muslims outside the occupied land had an obligation to help those under attack. "If the inhabitants of that area are not sufficient in number, fall short, or are lazy, the individually obligatory nature of jihad extends to those around them, and so on and so on until it covers the entire Earth, being individually obligatory (fard 'ayn) just like salat, fasting, and the like so that nobody may abandon it."[10]

Although focused for the team being on Afghanistan, Azzam's concept of jihad went much further. He considered the freeing of all Muslim lands from domination by non-Muslim a duty incumbent upon all believers. "The obligation of Jihad today remains *fard 'ayn* (an individual obligation of a believer)," he proclaimed, "until the liberation of the last piece of land which was in the hands of Muslims but has been occupied by the disbelievers."[11]

Azzam's preaching worked on bin Laden's conscience. Before the Afghan war, Osama does not seem to have considered anything other than the greater jihad. For him being a good Muslim meant prayer, personal piety, and resisting the temptations of the flesh. However, he had never been one to sit still. After listening to Azzam, he longed to take up the cause, but his family urged him not to go, and, for a while at least, he listened to them. Finally, religious zeal overcame doubt and the admonition of family, and he left for Afghanistan in 1984. "I feel so guilty for listening to my friends and those that I love to not come here [to Afghanistan] and stay home for reasons of safety," he confided to a Syrian journalist, "and I feel that this delay of four years requires my martyrdom in the name of God."[12] Despite his yearning for a glorious death, though, Osama did no go to fight the Soviets. Instead, he used his wealth to facilitate deployment of other mujahedeen to Afghanistan. In lat 1984 or early 1985, he, Azzam and Bodejema Bounoua set up the *Maktab al Khidmat lil Mujadidin al Arab*, the Afghan Service Bureau, an organization in Peshawar, Pakistan that helped Arab fighters join the insurgency. "We have found this bureau to gather the Arabs and to send them inside Afghanistan," Azzam declared. "We are here as servants. We are proud to serve the boots of the mujahideen inside Afghanistan."[13]

The Service Bureau helped recruit, transport, house, and pay Arab volunteers for the struggle with the Soviets. With his personal wealth, ties to the bin Laden group, and connections to the royal family and wealthy Saudis, bin Laden was too valuable to risk losing on the battlefield. Azzam preferred to use him as a recruiter, financer, and facilitator. More than a tenth of all private donations from Saudi donors to the Afghan cause went to bin Laden's organization.[14] The Service Bureau also published a propaganda magazine, *Jihad*, to recruit fighters and raise money throughout the Muslim world. Although he remained in the shadow of Azzam, bin Laden did earn a reputation for dedication and generosity. Abdullah Anas, an Algerian who worked with him in the Service Bureau, described bin Laden as a tireless "activist with great imagination" "He ate very little," Anas recalled. "He slept very little. Very generous. He'd give you his clothes. He'd give you his money."[15]

Bin Laden arrived fortuitously in Pakistan at the pivotal point when American and Saudi aid had begun to tip the balance of the war in favor of the Afghan insurgents. This serendipity led to the creation of a pervasive myth. Some Americans and many others outside the U.S. believe that the Central Intelligence Agency funded bin Laden's activities or even put him on its payroll. As long as Agency records remain classified, these rumors will persist. However, evidence in the public domain strongly suggests that no such relationship ever existed. To begin with, Osama bin Laden played a very minor role in the struggle. Few insurgent leaders had ever heard of him. While he may have been useful as a conduit for private funds, these funds made up but a small fraction of the money invested in supporting the Afghan cause. The CIA preferred to work through its Pakistani counterpart, the Inter-Services Intelligence Agency (ISI), which in turn distributed money to Afghan warlords fighting the Soviets. The Saudi government sent its funds through an even more circuitous route. It deposited $350-500 million a year in a Swiss bank account controlled by the U.S., which then funneled it to the Afghans via the ISI.[16] The Saudis also raised funds from private donors, but less than twenty percent of this money went to bin Laden.[17]

THE HOLY WARRIOR AND THE AFGHAN ARABS

While he demonstrated some proficiency in his supporting role, Osama was itching for more active participation in the jihad. He wanted to fight the Soviets and their Afghan puppet government directly. As with so many other aspects of his life, large gaps in the historical record obscure bin Laden's activities inside Afghanistan. All objective accounts, though, agree that he played a very minor role. With no military training or combat experience, he would have been of little use to the hardened Afghan commanders used to operating in the rugged terrain. Like celebrities visiting any war zone, bin Laden would have been a liability. Ill prepared to fight and yet too valuable to lose, he would have required protection, which meant detailing real fighters who could have been put to better use. While Bin Laden may have shown up at an insurgent camp, its commander probably would have kept him out of harms way.

If he wanted to fight, Osama would have to raise forces of his own to lead into battle. His personal wealth and family resources along with the ethnic makeup of the mujahedeen helped him achieve his goal. Most of the young men hanging around Peshawar came from various parts of the Arab world. They and bin Laden spoke Arabic but neither Pashtun (the language of the largest Afghan tribe) nor Urdu (the language of Pakistan). Like bin Laden, these Arab mujahedeen had little to offer the Afghan insurgents but their commitment to the struggle. Like him, they too were spoiling for a fight, but the insurgents had even less use for most of them than they did for the Saudi millionaire. Determined to enter the fray, bin Laden decided to form these men into an Arab force under his command. Acting independently, his "Afghan Arabs" could, bin Laden was certain, have a significant impact on the war. Barring that, they would at least achieve the martyrdom he and so many of them seemed to desire.

Osama's eagerness to form an Arab unit separate from the Afghans brought him first into disagreement and then into open conflict with Azzam. The charismatic Palestinian believed that the task of foreigners should be to fund, support, and otherwise aide the Afghan rebels. Anyone prepared to fight should attach himself to an Afghan unit. He no doubt also realized that a small force of fewer than a thousand untrained Arabs could accomplish little by themselves. Because he had ample personal resources, however, bin Laden could do what he wanted. No doubt Azzam also opposed the scheme because it would divert funds that would otherwise have gone to the Service Bureau had bin Laden not wasted them on his pet project.

Inserting themselves into the insurgency, Bin Laden and his followers adopted a classic guerrilla insurgent strategy: they would liberate one area and expand out of it to free more and more territory. They chose Jaji Maydan, a remote area in the mountains along the Pakistan border, near enough to trans-border routes to obtain supplies and far enough from any large Soviet force concentration to avoid destruction. Osama brought in Bin Laden Group construction equipment and, beginning in 1986, built a fortified camp, making use of existing caves within the area. He named the camp "Al-Masada" (the lion's den). One observer explained both bin Laden's plan and his choice of location. "Liberate one area and after that do liberation of other areas," he observed. "Jaji was chosen because of its geographical location—close to Parcahinar (a finger of Pakistani territory that extends into eastern Afghanistan)."[18] Bin Laden himself insisted that he had deliberately situated his camp so that it would be the first thing the Soviet forces saw when they entered the area and so they would have to attack it.[19] As usual, bin Laden exaggerated his importance in the scheme of things. The Lion's Den was but one small part of a major insurgent build up in the region. It did attract attention, but the Soviets were far more concerned about seasoned Afghan commanders and their large, experienced, and well equipped cadres than they were about bin Laden and his rag-tag bunch of Arab fighters.

Despite his bravado, neither bin Laden nor his Arab mujahedeen performed well on the battlefield. On April 17, 1987, he led 120 of his men in a raid on an Afghan Government outpost near the town of Khost, not far from the Lion's Den. Despite artillery support from Afghan Insurgent Commander, Gulbuddin Hekmatyar, the operation went poorly. The attacking Arabs had made insufficient logistical preparation, so that their attack force had to wait for ammunition, rockets, and mortars to be manhandled into position. Hungry soldiers found that their leaders had also neglected to pack sufficient quantities of food. At the last minute, they also realized that no one had brought the electrical wire to connect their rockets to the detonators. Finally, a single Afghan soldier spotted their clumsy preparations and held off the assault with a single machinegun.[20] The operation cost bin Laden and his Arabs what little credibility they had among the Afghan insurgents. A month later, he led another, more successful attack, but again, the number of fighters engaged suggests that the "battle" was little more than a skirmish. The operation also provoked the Soviets into bombarding the Lion's Den for several weeks, which killed many of the Afghan Arabs and forced bin Laden to temporarily abandon his camp.

An account published in an Egyptian weekly magazine described the low regard in which one insurgent commander, Ahmad Shah Massoud, held Osama and his Afghan Arabs. He considered the Afghan Arabs to be so disorganized that he refused to let them participate in operations with his forces. To the seasoned Afghan commander, these foreign Mujahedeen seemed more interested in seeking martyrdom for themselves than in defeating the Soviets. Massoud also considered bin Laden's motives to be obscure.[21] Ironically, a far more organized and focused bin Laden would approve the plan to kill Massoud just days before 9/11.

Although he was personally brave, Osama in no way contributed to the Afghan victory. Most of the "battles" in which he fought were minor skirmishes, or, if they were major battles, he and his Arab fighters played a minor role in them. Bin Laden's military reputation consists largely of smoke and mirrors. Properly employed, however, smoke and mirrors can produce a powerful illusion. Osama bin Laden's exploits grew more important with each telling and contributed greatly to an emerging bin Laden myth. He also drew the same conclusions about the Afghan War that the Americans had: it was a Soviet Vietnam.

The lesson of Vietnam re-enforced by the Afghan War against the Soviets and the American failure in Somalia would come to occupy a central place in bin Laden's thinking when declared war on the U.S. He concluded that despite their awesome conventional military might, the superpowers had great difficulty sustaining a protracted war. The Soviet army had been bled white in Afghanistan, and the victory had taught the mujahedeen an important lesson. "After our victory in Afghanistan and the defeat of the oppressors who had killed millions of Muslims, the legend about the invincibility of the superpowers vanished," bin Laden asserted in 1998. Vietnam had already demonstrated that America could also be defeated in an insurgency, but Somalia demonstrated that the U.S. would prove to be an even weaker opponent than the Soviet Union. "They [the mujahedeen] thought that the Americans were like the Russians, so they trained and prepared," Osama expounded. "They were stunned when they discovered how low was the morale of the American soldier. . . . He was unable to endure the strikes that were dealt his Army."[22] In this grandiloquent statement bin Laden exaggerated the role of the mujahedeen in both Afghanistan and Somalia and seriously underestimated the morale of the American soldier and the determination of the U.S. when its real interests were at stake. The foreign mujahedeen were too few and too incompetent to have affected the outcome of the Afghan war. The numbers in Somalia were even fewer in both absolute terms and as a percentage of total fighters. The U.S. did withdraw from Somalia following the disastrous effort to capture the warlord Mohammed Farah Aided, but that decision stemmed from lack of resolve on the part of the Clinton administration rather than poor morale among American soldiers. The public would probably have tolerated a sharp response to the Somalis even if it was not keen on a protracted war in a country in which no1 vital U.S. interests were at stake. Bin Laden would discover that when he attacked the American homeland, the response would be swift, terrible, and sustained.

AFGHAN CIVIL WAR

Soviet withdrawal from Afghanistan did not leave the country stable and at peace. Moscow left a puppet regime and military advisors to support an Afghan army that put up a decent fight against the insurgents. Far from unified except in hatred of the Soviet-backed regime, the rebels fought each other as they struggled to oust the Marxist government in Kabul. They captured the capital in 1992, and then fell to fighting among themselves. The civil war continued until 1996, when a Pashtun group (the Taliban) seized power. Even then, an alliance of northern Tajik and other tribes remained independent until the American invasion when they helped to overthrow the Taliban.

Osama bin Laden played as minor role in the fighting for control of Afghanistan as he had in the struggle to oust the Soviets. Far from covering himself in glory, he once again performed rather poorly. In 1989 he and his Afghan Arabs participated in the disastrous assault on Jalalabad. Government forces repulsed the attack inflicting heavy casualties on the mujahedeen. After lying low during several days of aerial bombardment, bin Laden and his forces slinked away. He soon left for Saudi Arabia. He would return to Afghanistan briefly and then move there to live in 1996. By then the country would be under the brutal rule of the religious fanatic,

Mullah Mohammed Omar, and bin Laden would head the world's most infamous terrorist organization.

TRIUMPH OF THE TALIBAN

In the Pashtun language *Taliban* means "religious student." The group that seized power in Afghanistan in 1996 had passed through *madrasas* during the 1980s and early 1990s. While "Madrasa" in Arabic simply means "school," the institutions these Afghans attended taught little more than memorizing the *Quran* and the tenets of radical Islamism. Most of the Imams who taught at these madrasas belonged to the neo-Deobandi movement. Deobandism shared with Wahabism an extremely conservative view of Islam. Islamic civilizations had fallen behind the West, the Deobandis maintained, because Muslim had lost touch with the core teachings and values of the Prophet Mohammed. The way to a better future lay through a return to the society of Islam's first century. The movement derived its name from the Quranic School in Deoband, India, which has trained South Asian imams during the past two centuries.[23] Though not inherently violent, Deobandism lent itself to further radicalization in the turbulent regions of Afghanistan and Pakistan. If true Islamic society could not be restored by prayer and righteous living, it must be restored by force. The Neo-Deobandi madrasa movement received a powerful boost from a massive infusion of Saudi cash. Concerned about the spread of radical Shi'a ideology following the Iranian revolution, the monarchy and private Saudi charities funded conservative madrasas all over the Muslim world. Saudi money and neo-Deobandist theology made for a volatile mix in the unstable conditions of Afghanistan and Pakistan.

A decade of war had produced an inexhaustible supply of recruits for radicalin madrasas that offered a free education, books, room and board, and in some cases, a stipend for their families. A generation of young Afghans had grown up in refugee camps in Pakistan. A significant number of these children had been orphaned by the conflict. They grew up to become exactly the sort of rootless, angry young men extremist organizations all over the world love to recruit. Under different circumstances these youths might have been recruited by street gangs or religious cults. In Pakistan's refugee camps they were grist for the jihadists' mill. Their leader Mullah Mohammed Omar had taught in one of the radical madrasas. Like Osama bin Laden he believed God had called him to special mission, and nothing would dissuade him from this conviction. He also shared bin Laden's conviction that the U.S. was responsible for all the ills of the Muslim world. "America controls the governments of the Islamic countries," Omar told a Voice of America Interviewer after the 9/11 attacks.

> The people ask to follow Islam, but the governments do not listen because they are in the grip of the United States. If someone follows the path of Islam, the government arrests him, tortures him or kills him. This is the doing of America. If it stops supporting those governments and lets the people deal with them, then such things won't happen. America has created the evil that is attacking it.[24]

The Taliban embrace an Islamist theology more extreme than that of Saudi Arabia's conservative Wahhabi clerics. They unleashed a religious reign of terror on Afghanistan. They enacted the strictest form of Sharia law. They prevented women from attending school. Covering female hair with a head scarf (hijab) or even the face with a veil did not satisfy them. Women had to remain indoors unless necessity required them to go out. Then they had to be covered from head to toe in the cumbersome light blue burqa, which offers very limited vision through mesh around the eyes. If possible, women who ventured out in public were to be accompanied by a male relative at all times. Men had to wear beards. The Taliban banned music, movies, and most television programs. The Taliban punished adultery with death by public stoning. They beheaded barbers who shaved beards and executed those guilty of a host of other crimes.

BIRTH OF THE BIN LADEN MYTH

The Afghan war against the Soviets and the ensuing civil war for control of the country created an enduring myth. The Afghan Arab leaders greatly exaggerated their role in the struggle. With no one to gainsay them, they were free to rewrite history. They turned their abysmal performance in the battle for Jalalabad into a stunning success. "The Arab brethren contributed greatly in these battles," boasted Afghan Arab Abu Salman.

"The Afghan commanders became dependent on them . . . [and the] Jalalabad battles proved the capabilities of Arab fighters, they participated in numerous liberation operations [sic]."[25] The small number of Arab fighters alone belies this exaggerated claim. A journalistic account from the time of the siege further contradicts the rosy assessment of the prowess of the Afghan Arabs. Edward Gardet, who visited bin Laden's camp with a group of Afghans in February 1989, describes a rather hostile exchange with the Saudi leader. Bin Laden demanded to know who the men were and why they had come. "This is our Jihad not your Jihad," the Afghans told Osama. "We've been coming here for quite a number of years, and we've never seen you guys," the journalist replied. As interpreters translated the heated Arabic exchange into Pashtun, the Afghans were "snickering. There was obviously no love lost between the two sides." Gardet concluded that bin Laden came across as "being a rather spoiled brat, like he was sort of 'playing at jihad.'" The journalist also commented on bin Laden's obsession with being noticed and respected.[26] Any further doubt about the uneasy relationship between the foreign mujahedeen and the Afghanis should be dispelled by the message bin Laden and his followers received following the Soviet withdrawal. Following the withdrawal of Soviet forces and defeat of the Marxist regime, the Afghan Arabs were told politely but firmly to go home. According to Ahmad Shah Ahmadzai (acting Afghan prime minister, 1995-96), the Afghans thanked the foreigners but asked them to leave rather than join with any of the factions vying for control of the country. Ahmadzai maintained that objection to the continued presence of the Afghan Arabs arose because of their support for the ultra-conservative Gulbuddin Hekmatyar.[27]

Fortunately for bin Laden, these accounts never circulated very far abroad and so did not damage his growing reputation. Although he remained largely unknown in the West, Osama bin Laden became something of a celebrity in Saudi Arabia and parts of the larger Arab world following the Afghan War. When he returned home, he found himself lionized by his countrymen eager to hear about his exploits in Afghanistan. In its fully developed form, the bin Baden myth gave Osama a messianic complex, a deep conviction that Allah had called him to a special mission and would bless his endeavours. Bin Laden even maintained that he and his Arab fighters, not the NATO alliance had won the Cold War. In a 1997 interview with CNN's Peter Arnett, bin Laden referred to "the collapse of the Soviet Union in which the US has no mentionable role, but rather the credit goes to God, Praise and Glory be to Him, and the Mujahedeen in Afghanistan."[28] The Arab street believed the myth and held bin Laden in high esteem. His popularity would grow in the Arab world as his infamy grew in the West. By 2004, 65% of Pakistanis, 55% of Jordanians, and 45% of Moroccans had a favorable view of Osama bin Laden.[29]

NOTES

1. "Soviet War in Afghanistan," available at http://www.absoluteastronomy.com/topics/Soviet_war_in_Afghanistan, accessed March 4, 2009.
2. Robert M. Cassidy, *Russia in Afghanistan and Chechnya: Military Strategic Culture and the Paradox of Asymmetry* (Carlisle Barracks, PA: Strategic Studies Institute, U.S. Army War College, 2003), p. 15.
3. "The CIA's Intervention in Afghanistan," *Le Nouvel Observateur*, Paris, 15-21 January 1998, available at http://www.globalresearch.ca/articles/BRZ110A.html, accessed March 5, 2009.
4. Steve Cole, *The Bin Ladens: An Arabian Family in the American Century* (New York: Penguin, 2008), pp. 301-303.
5. Jamal Khashoggi, cited in Peter Bergen, *The Osama bin Laden I Know* (New York: Free Press, 2006), p. 41.
6. Abdullah Azzam, *Defense of Muslim Lands*, available at http://www.religioscope.com/info/doc/jihad/azzam_defence_4_chap2.htm, accessed March 11, 2009.
7. Account of Jamal Ismail in Bergen, *The Osama bin Laden I Know*, p. 26.
8. Account of Jamal Khalifa, in ibid., pp. 27-28.
9. Abdullah Azzam, *Defense of Muslim Lands, the First Obligation of* Faith, available in translation at http://www.islamistwatch.org/texts/azzam/defense/chap3.html, accessed July 2, 2009.
10. Abdullah Azzam, *Join the Caravan*, 1988, available in translation at http://www.religioscope.com/info/doc/jihad/azzam_caravan_5_part3.htm, accessed July 2, 2009.
11. Quoted in Sherifa Zuhur, *A Hundred Osamas: Islamist Threats and the Future of Counterinsurgency*, (Carlisle Barracks, PA: Strategic Studies Institute, 2005), p. 30.
12. Basil Muhammad, quoted in ibid., p. 39.
13. Abdullah Azzam quoted by Boudejama Bounoua in ibid., p. 29.
14. Lawrence Wright, *The Looming Tower: Al-Qaeda and the Road to 9/11*. New York: Knopf, 2006), p. 104.
15. Ibid.

16. Ibid.
17. Ibid.
18. Jamal Ismail, quoted in Bergen, *The Osama bin Laden I Know*, p. 53.
19. Osama bin Laden, quoted, ibid., p. 52.
20. Wright, *Looming Tower*, p. 116.
21. "A Millionaire Finances Extremism in Egypt and Saudi Arabia," *Ruz al Yusuf*, date unknown, in Bergen, *Osama bin Laden I Knew*, p. 94.
22. Osama bin Laden, May 1998 statement, in Raymond Ibrahim, ed. and trans., *The Al Qaeda Reader* (New York: Broadway Books, 2007), p. 260.
23. Details on Deobandism from Global Security, http://www.globalsecurity.org/military/intro/islam-deobandi.htm, accessed May 25, 2009.
24. Mullah Mohammed Omar, Interview with Voice of America, in *The Guardian*, September 26, 2001, available at http://www.guardian.co.uk/world/2001/sep/26/afghanistan.features11, accessed July 2, 2001.
25. Michael Scheuer, *Through Our Enemies' Eyes: Osama bin Laden, Radical Islam, and the Future of America* (Washington, DC: 2007; first ed., 2006), pp. 111-112.
26. Edward Giardet, account in Bergen, *The Osama bin Laden I Know*, p. 90.
27. Ahmad Shah Ahmadai, quoted in Bergen, *The Osama bin Laden I Know*, p. 105.
28. Transcript of Osama bin Laden interview with Peter Arnett, March 1997, http://www.anusha.com/osamaint.htm, accessed May 1, 2009.
29. Pew Charitable Trust, *Global Attitudes Survey*, 2004, available at http://pewglobal.org/reports/display.php?ReportID=206, accessed June 5, 2009.

CHAPTER 4

AL-QAEDA

Most of the foreign fighters who journeyed to Afghanistan in the 1980s had a single purpose: to repel the Soviet invasion and overthrow the Communist regime in Kabul. When the war ended, they went home. The various Afghan warlords slugged it out for control of their war-ravaged country but thought no further than the limited goal of gaining power. For Osama bin Laden, however, the Afghan war was merely a beginning. The struggle had empowered him and, further, had made him aware of the plight of Muslims in other embattled lands. He had also grown accustomed to the notoriety the conflict had brought him, and he was perhaps reluctant to relinquish the limelight. Cooperating with other like-minded individuals, he transformed his Afghan Arab fighters from a guerrilla force into an organization and, more broadly, a movement.

AZZAM AND BIN LADEN

As the war drew to a close, Azzam and Osama looked beyond the immediate struggle to the plight of Muslims throughout the world. For bin Laden the Afghan war had focused bin Laden's piety and persuaded revealed in concrete terms the wisdom of Azzam's teaching. He wanted to continued jihad against the enemies of Islam where ever he found them. Perhaps he also missed the attention and exhilaration war provided him. In cooperation with other like-minded individuals, Azzam and bin Laden created al-Qaeda in the 1988. Although they agreed in principle on the broad goals of the new organization, the founders of al-Qaeda disagreed on one vital point. Azzam believed that the obligation to engage in jihad incumbent upon all Muslims applied only to foreign countries under occupation. Some of the Afghan Arabs, particularly those from Egypt, wished to overthrow what they considered apostate regimes ruling many Muslim countries while Azzam did not wish to fight other Muslims.[1] Azzam's conception of jihad did not extend beyond those lands in which non-Muslim regimes oppressed Muslim people:

> Jihad and the rifle alone: no negotiations, no conferences, no dialogues. . . . This duty will not end with victory in Afghanistan; jihad will remain an individual obligation until all other lands that were Muslim are returned to us so that Islam will reign again: before us lie Palestine, Bokhara, Lebanon, Chad, Eritrea, Somalia, the Philippines, Burma, Southern Yemen, Tashkent and Andalusia [southern Spain].[2]

His lengthy diatribe makes no mention of Egypt, Saudi Arabia, and the United States, all of which would eventually be targeted by al-Qaeda. Although he embraced the duty to liberate occupied Muslim lands, bin Laden does not seem to have made up his mind about the justice and legality of overthrowing Muslim governments. By all accounts he remained a loyal Saudi subject, recognizing that the monarchy and many wealthy Saudis were funding the Afghan jihad. In the coming years, however, he would come to accept the idea that apostate Muslims could be the target of jihad.

Although bin Laden and Azzam never formally parted company, relations between the two grew increasingly cool. This growing alienation developed out of a variety of complex factors. The major bone of contention between them remained Osama's determination to create an independent Arab force to wage jihad inside Afghanistan. Azzam considered the effort a waste of resources, but since Osama funded the effort out of his own pocket, Azzam could do nothing about it. Beneath the quarrel over creating this independent force lay a deeper tension. Egyptian radicals made up a disproportionate number of the Afghan Arabs, particularly its leadership. Many of the Egyptian Mujahedeen had broken from the Muslim Brotherhood, which they considered too willing to work with the hated Egyptian government. Azzam distrusted these men. He also feared the loss of bin Laden's money for own initiatives. For these reasons, he sought to reduce their presence in al-Qaeda. Azzam advocated a selection process for membership, but bin Laden disagreed.[3]

Azzam's fears were well founded. Bin Laden gave the Egyptian group al-Jihad, which had broken with the Muslim Brotherhood, $100,000 to set up its own camp. Although author Richard Wright argues that this award signaled bin Laden's tilt towards the Egyptians, it seem more likely that he was still hedging his bet.[4] The al-Jihad camp was one of several established by bin Laden. He had even founded one Arab camp jointly with Azzam, who may have been persuaded that an all-Arab group did have some merits.[5]

Personal issues may also have contributed to bin Laden's growing coolness towards his former mentor. Azzam was an internationally recognized Muslim scholar while bin Laden had little more than a high school degree. In college he studied economics, not theology. Bin Laden may have suffered from an inferiority complex in Azzam's presence. For his part, Azzam may have been patronizing and condescending towards bin Laden, treating him as a follower, not an equal. Azzam's widow referred to this potential source of tension. She described Osama as "not very educated. He holds a high school degree. . . . It is true that he gave lectures to *ulema* and *sheikhs*, but he was easy to persuade."[6]

Despite their differences, the real threat to Azzam came not from bin Laden but from the Egyptians. In 1989, Azzam and his two sons were murdered in Peshawar, Pakistan. The crime has never been solved. Most experts agree that bin Laden was not involved in the murder. Ahmad Zaidan, who wrote an Arabic language book about bin Laden based on his interviews with the man, dismissed the idea that Osama had anything to do with killing Azzam. "Osama bin Laden, he's not the type of person to kill Abdullah Azzam," Zaidan insisted. "Otherwise, if he be exposed [sic], he would be finished, totally."[7] Former CIA Middle East analyst Bruce Riedel concludes that Azzam was probably the victim of the "internecine fighting within the mujahedeen movement and among the Arabs congregated around it in Pakistan." He also notes that Azzam and the Egyptian radical Ayman Zawahiri competed for bin Laden's support and money.[8] Other sources corroborate this competition.

BIRTH OF AL-QAEDA

Al-Qaeda, Arabic for the "the base," grew out of the *Maktab al Khidmat lil Mujadidin al Arab* ("Afghan Service Bureau," MAK), founded in 1984 or 1985 by bin Laden and Azzam to facilitate recruitment and travel of foreign *mujahedeen* to fight the Soviets in Afghanistan. Several accounts document the formation of al-Qaeda, although they do not always agree on specific details. Bin Laden himself provides one account. "Abu Ubaidah al Banjshiri established the training camps against Russia's terrorism during the 1980s," he observed. "We used to call the training camp al Qaeda. And the name stayed."[9] In an April 1988 article in his *Jihad* magazine, Azzam provided a fuller explanation of the organization:

> Every principle needs a vanguard to carry it forward and, while forcing its way into society, puts with heavy tasks and enormous sacrifices. There is no ideology, neither earthly nor heavenly, that does not require such a vanguard that gives everything it possesses in order to achieve victory for the ideology. It carries the flag all along the sheer endless and difficult path until it reaches its destination. The vanguard constitutes the solid base (al Qaeda Sulbah) for the expected society.[10]

Captured documents reveal that the idea of broadening al-Qaeda's mandate may have come from Ayman al Zawahiri's Islamic Jihad organization. "This future project is in the interest of the Egyptian brothers," remarked Abu al Rida to bin Laden in an August 1988 meeting.[11] Zawahiri would continue to play a major role in al-Qaeda down to the present, so much so that some analysts consider him the brain of al-Qaeda even though bin Laden is its heart and spiritual leader. The account of an early Saudi recruit supports the conclusion that the idea for al-Qaeda originated with Egyptian radicals. "The establishment of al Qaeda was discussed in the home of Osama bin Laden in Peshawar following the departure of the Russians from Afghanistan and the end of the Jihad," reported Hasan Abd-Rabbuh. "I was one of those who witnessed the birth of al Qaeda. The idea of al Qaeda is an Egyptian one by the Islamic Jihad group led by Abu-Ubaidah al Banjshiri and Abu-Hafs."[12]

Al Banjishiri explained to this young recruit the goal of this new organization and bin Laden's role in its creation. "You are aware of brother Osama bin Laden's generosity," the Egyptian said.

> He has spent a lot of money to buy arms for the young mujahedeen as well as in training them and paying for their travel tickets. We should not waste this. We should invest in these young men and we should mobilize them under his umbrella. We should form an Islamic army for jihad that will be called al Qaeda. This army will be one of the fruits of what bin Laden has spent on the Afghan jihad. We should train these young men and equip them to be ready to uphold Islam and defend Muslims in any part of the world. The members of this army should be organized and highly trained.[13]

In its early days, al-Qaeda did not yet have the global agenda it later acquired. It had not even focused on Muslim failing to rule by strict *sharia* law, although its Egyptian members certainly desired to remove the hated regime of President Hosni Mubarak. One of bin Laden's associates recounts the first time the Saudi millionaire broached the idea for a permanent jihadist group. "Osama believed he could set up an army of young men responding to the jihad call," recalled Abu Mahmud. "When he presented the idea to us, he did not speak of jihad against Arab regimes, but of helping Muslims against the infidel government oppressing them, as was the case in Palestine, the Philippines, and Kashmir, especially Central Asia, which was under Soviet rule then."[14]

ORGANIZATION

Al-Qaeda soon developed into a formal organization with a hierarchy of leaders and a series of committees. Bin Laden emerged as its leader, although he may have initially been reluctant to accept the job. According to his brother-in-law, the rather humble and unassuming Osama had to be persuaded to accept the position.[15] The founders set up five standing committees to run the organization: a Military Committee that ran training camps and procured weapons, an Islamic Study Committee that issued *fatwas* (religious decrees) and rulings, a Media Committee that published Newspapers, a Travel Committee that took care of passports, visas, and tickets, and a Finance Committee that raised money. A ruling *shura* (council) oversaw the work of the committees.[16] Eventually, al-Qaeda evolved into a more decentralized organization with regional bureaus linked to cells with 2-15 members each. Some cells had specialized responsibilities while others were created for a single terrorist operation.[17]

Al-Qaeda benefits by the folklore that had enveloped the Afghan Arabs. Following the Soviet withdrawal from Afghanistan, the number of foreign Mujahideen journeying to the country actually increased, attracted no doubt by stories of the great jihadist victory there and anxious to help overthrow the communist puppet government the Soviets had left behind in Kabul. Not all of these young men were acceptable to al-Qaeda. The new organization had to develop membership standards and training protocols. The *Shura* laid down specific requirements for membership. Applicants had to make an open-ended commitment to the organization. They had to be obedient, well-mannered, and agree to obey all of al-Qaeda's statutes and instructions. They also had to be referred by someone already in the organizations that al-Qaeda's leaders knew and trusted.[18] Initial acceptance did not guarantee a membership. Recruits entered "a testing camp and [the] best brothers of them are chosen to enter Al Qaeda Al Askariya (the military base)."[19] According to one recruit, initial training lasted two weeks during which instructors carefully screened applicants. "They looked for certain specific qualifications among these young men," he reported. "The most important criteria is that the ones who are chosen should be young, zealous, obedient, and with a weak character that obeys instructions without question."[20] These criteria define the generic profile of recruits to almost any terrorist organization or religious cult, for that matter.

Al-Qaeda attracted far more recruits than it could absorb, but it turned very few volunteers away. Of the thousands of men who passed through its training camps, only a small percentage stayed with the main organization in Afghanistan. Some of those not admitted were sent to fight in the conflicts in Bosnia, Chechnya, and Kashmir, but the vast majority returned to their own countries to await further instructions from bin Laden and the Shura. They would become the nuclei of al-Qaeda's worldwide network of cells. Estimates of the number of those trained in al-Qaeda camps between 1989 and 2001 vary widely, ranging from 10,000-110,000. No more than 3000 of these volunteers joined al-Qaeda itself.[21] Most of the trainees came from Arab countries. While no complete registry of them has yet been found, the Pakistani government during the 1990s asked foreign *mujahedeen* in their country to register with the authorities. The registry for Pakistan's Northwest Frontier Province, immediately adjacent to Afghanistan, provides a rough indication of the number of foreign fighters by country of origin: "1,142 were Egyptian; 981 Saudis; 946 Sudanese; 792 Algerians; 771 Jordanians; 326 Iraqis; 292 Syrians; 234 Sudanese; 199 Libyans; 117 Tunisians; and 102 Moroccans."[22]

The al-Qaeda organization headquartered in Afghanistan during the 1990s might be compared to a multi-national corporation. Its leadership, committees, camps, and permanent cadres in Afghanistan comprised the corporate head office. Al-Qaeda central also commanded a global network of cells in 76 countries by 2001.[23] In addition to its permanent cells, al-Qaeda also recruited local operatives within countries in which it carried out attacks. These local recruits, who had never been to Afghanistan, performed routine tasks that would have exposed the foreign terrorist specialists (such as bomb makers) brought in for an operation to capture by local authorities. The 1998 bombing of the US embassy in Darussalam, Tanzania illustrates how Al-Qaeda combined such local recruits with professional operatives to carry out a mission. The organization recruited Khalfan Khamis Mohamed in a local mosque and won him to over to the jihadist cause. Once they were sure of his loyalty, they told him he would take part in an important mission, but they kept him in the dark as to its details. The foreign operatives in the cell asked Mohamed to rent the safe house the group needed and to buy the truck that would carry the explosives. As a local Tanzanian he could perform these tasks inconspicuously. The cell brought in an expert to build the bomb, but this specialist and the rest of the foreign operatives left the country before Mohamed drove the truck to the embassy on the day of the attack.[24] He may not even have known the target until the day of the attack. Perhaps the planners even intended him to be killed by the bomb. "We, the East Africa cell members, do not want to know about the operations plan since we are just implementers," proclaimed a document found on a computer seized in Tanzania after the attack.[25] Terrorist organizations have long maintained security by keeping local cells ignorant of the larger organization and providing individual cell members just enough information for them to carry out their portion of the operation.

Since 9/11, U.S. counter-terrorism operations have concentrated on denying al-Qaeda safe havens and on targeting its leadership. In his 2002 book, Rohan Gunaratna, one of the world's leading authorities on al-Qaeda, argued that "the most effective state response would be to target Al-Qaeda's leadership, cripple its command and control, and disrupt its current and future support bases."[26] This approach might have been effective before 9/11 when al-Qaeda was still a considerably more centralized organization, but even then such a "decapitation strike" would have left most of the terrorist network intact. However, al-Qaeda consists of much more than its head office. It exists on two other, far more menacing levels: a network of linked organizations and an ideological movement spread via the Internet both of which are very hard to disrupt.

AL-QAEDA THE NETWORK

If al-Qaeda worked like an international corporation with headquarters and branch offices, it also functioned as a conglomerate, a sort of holding company linking many terrorist organizations under its broad ideological umbrella. Analysts have also described it as a "network of networks," a vast global spider web of extremist groups united through radical Islamism and committed to attacking what it deems apostate Muslim regimes, the U.S., and America's European allies.

The al-Qaeda network developed further during bin Laden's years in Sudan. In 1995 an Islamic People's Conference met in Khartoum, Sudan. The conference brought together militants from Algeria, Pakistan, Jordan, Eritrea, Egypt, Yemen, Tunisia, and the Philippines. Al-Qaeda forged links with Hamas, Palestinian Islamic Jihad, and perhaps even Lebanese Hezbollah, a Shi'a group once considered incompatible with the Sunni extremists.[27] In Febuary1998, Osama bin Laden announced the formation of a new conglomerate: "The World Islamic Front for Jihad against Jews and Crusaders." Many known terrorist leaders from groups in Egypt, Pakistan and Bangladesh signed the alliance agreement, but bin Laden kept the identities of most of the organizations gathered under the new umbrella secret to protect them.[28]

Following the US invasion of Afghanistan in the wake of 9/11, this association along with al-Qaeda's own global network of cells grew in importance. The affiliates and branch offices carried on the struggle while al-Qaeda central rebuilt itself in Pakistan. As bin Laden relocated to the remote southeast border region of Afghanistan and Pakistan, his capacity to control or even influence the course of the terrorist campaign abroad was temporarily disrupted. This disruption of the headquarters in Afghanistan made it more difficult for al-Qaeda to move personnel and resources around its global network and to concentrate them for an operation like the 1998 embassy bombings. The network has, however, picked up the slack as local cells or affiliates organized, funded, and conducted operations such as the 2004 Madrid and 2005 London bombings. These cells may have enjoyed some support and guidance from the central organization, but they recruited locally and enjoyed considerable independence in carrying out their operations.

AL-QAEDA THE IDEOLOGICAL MOVEMENT

Considerable evidence suggests that al-Qaeda has continued to evolve beyond even the network level. Terrorism analyst Michael Chandler describes what he calls "third generation" terrorism. Bin Laden and his *shura*, the "first generation," directed operations from Afghanistan until the American invasion disrupted their central organization. This invasion sent first-generation al-Qaeda members fleeing back to their countries of origin. There they rejoined existing cells and organizations or set up new ones, recruiting the "second generation" of terrorists. In addition to these affiliates, the last few years have seen the rise of new, "third generation" groups whose members have no experience of Afghanistan or even a direct connection to those who trained in terrorist camps there. Al-Qaeda central provides inspiration and guidance and perhaps some support but probably does not exercise complete control of the new local groups. Third-generation terrorists may constitute themselves into their own local groups, raise their own funds, plan, and even conduct operations and only then link up with or at least seek the approval of the parent organization.[29] In response to President George Bush's assertion that any state not with the U.S. was with the terrorists, al-Qaeda seemed to say, "anyone who is against the U.S., is with us."

Even more ominous than this cancerous spread of al-Qaeda through direct recruitment by terrorist camp graduates is the spread of radical ideology via the Internet. Despite their intense dislike of Western secularism and democracy, bin Laden and his followers have readily adopted the technological tools of the culture they hate. The communications revolution has reached into the most remote corners of the globe. An astounding 1.6 billion of the world's 6.7 billion people have Internet access.[30] Six out of ten people on earth (4.1 billion) use cell phones.[31] Solar panels power satellite televisions for people without access to reliable electricity. These statistics have profound implications. People who are illiterate can access a wealth of online video and audio content. Communities that lack clean water, adequate food, healthcare and jobs can log on to the Internet and make international calls using their mobile telephones. Access to the overwhelming amount of information on the Internet can have a very destabilizing effect. Al-Qaeda's pronouncements about the decadence of the West and its spread to the non-Western world are made manifest by material that can be viewed online. Pornography, crass materialism, and subversive ideas abound, and the ease of accessing them validates for the Islamists their conclusion that Western secularism does indeed threaten traditional Islamic societies. The Internet also highlights the gap between the haves and the have-nots of the world, showing the poor and marginalized how much they lack.

In addition to facilitating extremism through its destabilizing effects, the communications revolution has made it easier for al-Qaeda and its affiliates to mobilize and focus the anger that the destabilization generates. Previously an angry young man had to be recruited personally by other terrorists. Now he need only log on to discover that he belongs to a global community of like-minded individuals. A host of websites preach al-Qaeda's extreme version of Islam to convince the alienated young adult living in Amsterdam, Berlin, Paris, London, or Minneapolis that all his problems stem from the Godless culture that surrounds and yet rejects him. Only by signing up for the jihadist cause and working to restore the *uma* of true Muslim believers can he free himself and his community from such oppression. Through the Internet the terrorist recruit can perhaps locate a local cell or al-Qaeda affiliate. The local group that he joins can then find detailed bombing making instructions and valuable information on suitable targets and their vulnerabilities, all online. His cell might even receive financial help via phony online charities that raise money for al-Qaeda. The cost of terrorist attacks is so low, however, that the young recruit and his associates may raise the money simply by pooling their resources or by engaging in petty crimes like credit card fraud.

FUNDING AND FINANCING

Like any organization al-Qaeda needs money. Terrorist funding refers to raising money to conduct a specific operation while terrorist financing refers to raising money for the day to day operations of the terrorist organization. Operational expenses are similar to those for any organization and institution and include personnel costs (paying salaries and benefits), supplies, publicity, etc. Conducting individual terrorist attacks is relatively cheap; financing a terrorist organization and its worldwide network of cells and affiliates is considerably more expensive. Some analysts estimate al-Qaeda's pre-9/11 operating budget to have been $30 million per year.[32] The London Underground bombings cost a few hundred British pounds, the 2004 Madrid train bombings cost around $10,000, and the 9/11 attacks cost as much as $500,000 dollars, provide by the main al-Qaeda organization in Pakistan.[33] The leader of the Madrid attacks funded that operation out of proceeds from his drug business, but the London bombers could pay for their attacks out of their own pockets. Al-Qaeda central, of course, funded 9/11.

Al-Qaeda has had numerous sources of income during its twenty-year history. During its early days bin Laden probably funded it himself out of his considerable personal fortune. He also received donations from wealthy Saudis and other supporters throughout the Muslim world. Islamic charities provided an additional source of revenue. Many contributors to these charities had no idea that their money was financing terrorism. Two legitimate businesses dealing in Honey also funneled their profits to al-Qaeda.[34]

Local cells and affiliates financed their activities and funded specific missions through criminal activity such as credit card fraud and identity theft.

Narcotics trafficking currently provides the greatest source of revenue for both al-Qaeda and the Taliban. Opium poppy cultivation in Afghanistan has increased dramatically since the fall of the Taliban, rising from under 50,000 hectares in 2001 to more than 150,000 hectares in 2008.[35] Afghanistan now produces about 75% of the world's opium.[36] Neither group produces or sells illegal drugs. They make their money by taxing opium cultivation, heroine production, and drug smuggling. NATO estimates that the Taliban get 40 to 60% of their income from narcotics.[37] With Afghanistan now producing more than 80 percent of the world heroine supply, this revenue sources is incredibly lucrative.

Countering terrorist financing is extremely difficult given al-Qaeda's numerous sources of revenue and the easy of moving money around the globe. Terrorism analysts disagree on whether to freeze and seize terrorist assets or to follow the money trail in an effort to garner intelligence on the terrorist organization. Both approaches have merit and should be employed in tandem. The low cost of terrorist operations make it seem that no counter-funding/financing strategies will be effective. The difficulty al-Qaeda has had in mounting operations against the U.S. and Western Europe during the past five years, however, suggests that the West has had some success in disrupting terrorist financing.

BIN-LADEN'S ROLE

Osama bin Laden's precise role in al-Qaeda during the first decade of its existence is n not entirely clear. He was, of course, the organization's titular leader and public face. He also provided much of the financial resources that funded its activities, contributing money from his personal fortune and raising it from wealthy Saudi donors. Both the Afghans and the Arabs wanted bin Laden's money, but they had serious reservations about his abilities. They competed for his support and deferred to him as necessary, but it is not clear how much they trusted his judgment or actually allowed him to make decisions.

One mujahedeen commander gave a candid appraisal of Osama bin Laden during the early days of al-Qaeda. "To be honest we didn't care about bin Laden," declared Haji Deen Mohamed. "We didn't notice him much. The only thing he did have was cash. The only thing was that he was rich."[38] If they coveted his wealth, the various factions thought far less of bin Laden's abilities in al-Qaeda's early days. A member of the Services Office provided a scathing comment on bin Laden's organizing ability:

> Osama, he had to create an organization and to keep everything under his control, but as an organizer, I think he had many mistakes during this period. In 1991 he had a project to enter Kabul and he spent 100 million rupees (more than 1.5 million dollars) and after a few weeks, everything collapsed and the people took his 100 million rupees. Osama as an organizer—completely a catastrophe, I consider him.[39]

The low opinion in which some Afghan leaders held the Saudi millionaire is further indicated by what happened when bin Laden returned to Afghanistan in 1992. He quickly discovered that his beloved Arab fighters had been incorporated into Afghan units and that he no longer controlled them. "I remember the people who were with Hekmatyar warned Osama," Abdullah Anas, Azzam's son-in-law remembered. "You are not anymore a leader. And after that, he immediately decided to go to Sudan."[40] Taliban and al-Qaeda expert Ahmed Rashid provides an accurate if unflattering portrait of bin Laden during these years:

> Arab Afghans who knew him during the jihad say he was neither intellectual nor articulate about what needed to be done in the Muslim world. In that sense he was neither the Lenin of the Islamic revolution, nor was he the international ideologue of the Islamic revolution such as Che Guevera was to the revolution in the third world. Bin Laden's former associates describe him as deeply impressionable, always in need of mentors, men who knew more about Islam and the modern world than he did.[41]

THE EMERGING LEADER

These critical assessments of Osama bin Laden during the al-Qaeda's early days do not diminish his importance to the movement in the long run. Without his personal fortune and ability to raise money, the organization might never have been formed and, even if it had, would not have progressed very far. In 1992, he was only thirty-five. Unlike his older brothers he had very little experience living or even traveling outside Saudi Arabia. Nor had he been given major assignments in the Bin Laden Group, the conglomerate created by his eldest brother Salem, which might have provided him greater managerial experience. Before joining the Afghan jihad, he had lived a very sheltered life among the Saudi elite.

Afghanistan had, however, profoundly changed bin Laden. "What I lived in two years there," he later reflected. "I could not have lived in a hundred years elsewhere."[42] This reflection suggests that he got an emotional high from danger and military activity, which he would miss when he returned to his ordinary life. During the next decade he would find that he need jihad and the exhilaration and notoriety it brought him. He would also grow into the role of international terrorist leader as his organization developed. While he might never be the brains of the al-Qaeda, he would be its heart and soul, inspiring a vast, complex international Islamist extremist network to make war against the most powerful nation on earth.

In 1992, however, these developments lay in an uncertain future, which might have unfolded quite differently. Osama left Afghanistan elated by the experience of war but demoralized about the future of jihad. His worldview developed considerably but was still largely unformed. He believed in the commitment to engage in jihad on behalf of Muslims in lands occupied by infidels, but he had not yet accepted that apostate regimes must be removed. He spoke of the Palestinian cause, but was unwilling to become directly involved in that struggle.[43] He seriously considered continuing jihad against the Soviet Union in its Central Asian Muslim republics, fighting the Indians on behalf of the Muslims of Kashmir, or the government of the Philippines on behalf of its Muslim minority.[44]

Ultimately, he decided to return to the land of his birth. Despite his mixed record and the minor role he had played in the Afghan War against the Soviets and the subsequent Afghan civil war, he arrived home to hero's welcome. After a brief stint on the speaking circuit in Saudi Arabia, he might have reverted to the quiet life of a younger brother in the family business. Once again, however, world events energized his religious zeal and focused his anger not only on unfaithful Muslim governments but also on the great Satan across the Atlantic.

NOTES

1. Peter Bergen, *The Osama bin Laden I Know* (New York: Free Press, 2006), p. 74.
2. John Esposito, *Unholy War: Terror in the Name of Islam* (Oxford, UK: Oxford University Press, 2002), p. 7.
3. Steve Coll, *The Bin Ladens: An Arabian Family in the American Century* (New York: Penguin, 2008), p. 355.
4. Lawrence Wright, *The Looming Tower: Al-Qaeda and the Road to 9/11* (New York: Knopf, 2006), p. 138.
5. Coll, *Bin Ladens*, pp. 334-335.
6. Quote and previous discussion in this paragraph from, ibid., p. 336.
7. Ahmad Zaidan, quoted in Bergen, *Osama bin Laden I Knew*, p. 97.
8. Brian Riedel, *Search for Al-Qaeda: Its Leadership, Ideology, and Future* (Washington, DC: Brookings Institute), 2008, p. 45.
9. Osama bin Laden interview with Taysir Alouni, Al Jazeera, October 2001, cited in Bergen, *Osama bin Laden I Know*, p. 74.
10. Abdullah Azzam, "Al Qaeda al Sulbah," *Jihad*, 41 (April 1988), excerpted in ibid., p. 75.
11. Transcript of conversation between Abu al Rida and Osama bin Laden, August 11, 1988, excerpted in ibid., p. 78.
12. Account of Hasan Abd-Rabbuh al Surayhi in ibid., p. 83.
13. Ibid., p. 83.
14. Abu Mahmud, quoted in Michael Scheuer, *Through Our Enemies' Eyes: Osama bin Laden, Radical Islam, and the Future of America* (Washington, DC: Potomac Books, 2007), p. 110.
15. Account of Jamal Kalifa, quoted in ibid., p. 81.
16. Description of al-Qaeda structure from Jessica Stern, *Terror in the Name of God: Why Religious Militants Kill* (New York: Harper Collins, 2003), p. 250.
17. Rohan Gunaratna, *Inside Al Qaeda: Global Network of Terror* (New York: Columbia University Press, 2002), p. 10.

18. Captured al-Qaeda document, reproduced in ibid., p. 81.
19. Ibid.
20. Account of Hasan Abd-Rabbuh al Surayhi in ibid., p. 84.
21. Ibid., p. 8.
22. Esposito, *Holy War, Inc.*, p. 90.
23. Gunaratna, *Inside Al Qaeda*, p. 79.
24. Account based on that given by Jessica Stern, *Terror in the Name of God: Why Religious Militants Kill* (New York: Harper Collins, 2003), pp. 239-45. Stern had access to classified evidence from Mohamed's trial.
25. Esposito, *Holy War, Inc.*, p. 30.
26. Ibid., p. 13.
27. Ibid., p. 85; Stern, *Terror in the Name of God*, p. 253.
28. Gunaratna, *Inside Al Qaeda*, p. 45.
29. Michael Chandler, "The Global Threat from Trans-national Terrorism: How it is Evolving and its Impact in Europe," presentation at the George C. Marshall Centre for Security Studies Conference on NATO and the EU Strategies Against Terrorism, July 19-21. 2005.
30. Internet World Status, http://www.internetworldstats.com/stats.htm, accessed May 12, 2009.
31. "World's poor drive growth in global cellphone use," *USA Today*, March 2, 2009, http://www.usatoday.com/tech/news/2009-03-02-un-digital_N.htm, accessed May 12, 2009.
32. Victor Comas, "Al Qaeda Financing and Funding to Affiliate Groups," *Strategic Insights*, IV, no. 1 (January 2005), available at http://www.ccc.nps.navy.mil/si/2005/Jan/comrasJan05.asp, accessed July 1, 2009.
33. Michael Buchanan, "London Bombs Cost Just Hundreds," BBC Online, January 3, 2006, available at http://news.bbc.co.uk/2/hi/uk_news/4576346.stm, accessed July 7, 2009.
34. Comas, "Al Qaeda Financing and Funding."
35. UN Office on Drugs and Crime, *World Drug Report 2009,* p. 35, available at http://www.unodc.org/unodc/en/data-and-analysis/WDR-2009.html, accessed July 7, 2009.
36. Ibid., p. 35.
37. Jerome Starkey, "Drugs for guns: how the Afghan heroin trade is fuelling the Taliban insurgency," *The Independent* (UK), April 29, 2008, available at http://www.independent.co.uk/news/world/asia/drugs-for-guns-how-the-afghan-heroin-trade-is-fuelling-the-taliban-insurgency-817230.html, accessed July 7, 2009.
38. Haji Deen Mohammed, quoted in Bergen, *Osama bin Laden I Knew*, p. 105.

39. Abdullah Anas in ibid., p. 104.
40. Ibid., p. 106.
41. Esposito, *Unholy War: Terror in the Name of Islam* (Oxford, UK: Oxford U. Press, 2002), p. 11
42. Ibid., p. 9.
43. Wright, *Looming Tower*, p. 131.
44. Ibid., p. 131.

CHAPTER 5

FIGHTING THE GREAT SATAN

Osama bin Laden emerged from the Afghan war against the Soviets with a powerful sense of mission but no clear focus. He had helped create an organization with international membership and potentially global reach. However, that organization was still very loose and lacked direction. Bin Laden did enjoy considerable notoriety and still possessed charisma and wealth. Perhaps more important he had constructed a powerful myth that he had probably come to believe himself, a deeply held conviction that foreign mujahedeen using his money, inspired by his zeal, and enjoying Allah's blessing had defeated the mighty Soviet empire. Osama had also had accepted the general principle that he should continue to jihad any and all who oppressed Islam anywhere in the world. Despite this conviction, however, he lacked direction. Where should he next employ his talents, resources, and experience?

IN SEARCH OF JIHAD

The world of the early 1990s afforded many possibilities for bin Laden to employ his talents, resources and experiences. The end of the Cold War and subsequent collapse of the Soviet Union created power vacuums all over the world, many of them in Muslim lands. The East African country of Somalia with its large Muslim population became the icon of a new post-Cold War phenomenon—the failed state. Yugoslavia disintegrated as three of its component republics seceded from the federation. Slovenia with homogenous Roman Catholic population left first and with virtually no violence. Croatia seceded next, but Serbia intervened to seize predominantly Serb areas, which it held for fours years. Bosnia with the most heterogeneous population of all the Yugoslav republics voted for secession and immediately descended into civil war. Bosnia's Muslim population faced ethnic cleansing as Bosnian Serbs drove them from territory they claimed through the systematic use of rape, murder, and torture. Then Muslims and Croats fell to fighting among themselves. The Soviet Muslim republic of Chechnya with its Muslim population wanted the independence the Soviet Union had granted to the Baltic states, Ukraine, and Georgia. Moscow refused to comply and sent in what remained of its army to conduct a brutal and largely ineffective counterinsurgency campaign against Chechen rebels. In the Philippines a Muslim separatist movement had fought a desultory war against the government in Manila for decades. Pakistan continued to send irregulars into Indian Kashmir to stir up unrest among its Muslim population. Some Afghan Arabs went off to fight in these conflicts, although according to one of his supporters, bin Laden did not order them to participate in these conflicts.[1] None of these endeavors fired his imagination as the Afghan jihad had done, perhaps because they lacked the worldwide attention of the Afghan struggle. Osama enjoyed notoriety as much as he embraced jihad.

Fortunately for him, a conflict much closer to home presented itself within a year of his return. His offer to form a Muslim army to liberate Kuwait from Saddam Hussein and its rejection by the Saudi monarchy stung bin Laden. It also helped crystallize his thinking. The real obstacles to recreating the *uma* (community of believers) of Islam's early days were the apostate regimes of countries such as Egypt and Saudi Arabia. They were the "near enemy." Behind them stood the United States with its military might and vast financial resources, the "far enemy," whose influence had to be driven from Muslim lands so that the near enemies could be defeated.

When he returned a hero from Afghanistan in 1989, however, these developments were not even on the horizon. The Afghan experience had changed him. For one thing, he had developed a definite anti-American rhetoric, although it had not yet turned violent. His main grievance like that of many in the Arab world was U.S. support for Israel. "The Americans won't stop their support of the Jews in Palestine," he proclaimed, "until we give them a lot of blows. They won't stop until we do jihad against them." At this point in his life bin Laden appears to have been speaking figuratively. "What is required is to wage an economic war against America," he went on to explain. "We have to boycott all American products. . . . They're taking the money we pay them for their products and giving it to the Jews to kill our brothers."[2]

Bin Laden also voiced criticism of the Saudi regime, which he had not done before his Afghan sojourn. Saudi Arabia was an Islamist state, but it did not conform to the jihadist ideal of how Muslims should be governed. They advocated an Islamic Republic governed by religious elders supporting a leader through the principle of consultation or "shura," not a monarchy. He also found fault with the less than pious behavior of the royal family, which included hundreds of princes and wealthy hangers-on living lavish lifestyles. Meanwhile, the majority of Saudis lived modest lives while a vast underclass of foreign workers had a low standard of living.

SOUTH YEMEN

Soon after he arrived home, bin Laden became embroiled in another jihad. South Yemen at the tip of the Arabian Peninsula had been a communist state since British withdrawal from its colony there in 1967. A small group of insurgents sought to overthrow the government, and Osama wanted to support them. Family history strengthened his moral conviction. His father had come from the remote Hadramut region of South Yemen, and Osama had turned his attention to the anti-communist struggle even before he left Afghanistan. According to one of his associates, bin Laden believed that after their success in against the Soviets, the Afghan Arabs should be employed to liberate South Yemen.[3]

Bin Laden approached the Chief of Saudi Intelligence Prince Turki offering to send al-Qaeda fighters into South Yemen to support the rebels. He would even help fund the operation. The prince later claimed that he turned bin Laden down flat. "I advised him at the time that that was not an acceptable idea," Turki recalled. However, Richard Clarke, terrorism expert in the Clinton administration, maintains that Turki had actually asked bin Laden "to organize a fundamentalist religion-based resistance to the communist-style regime."[4] Steve Riedel, a former CIA specialist on the Middle East, maintains that Saudi government wanted to overthrow the communists in Yemen, but that "it did not want a private army doing its bidding."[5] Whatever transpired between the leader of al-Qaeda and the head of Saudi intelligence became moot when the Cold War ended. North and South Yemen reunited peacefully in May 1990. Bin Laden did not like the arrangement, which incorporated former communists into the new government, and continued to fund rebel activity without permission from the Saudi government. His defiance of the monarchy brought a swift and harsh response. Interior minister Prince Nayif bin Abdul Aziz, a full brother of the king, called bin Laden into his office and ordered him to cease his activities at once, and confiscated his passport.[6]

THE GULF WAR

Bin Laden had little time to brood about this official rebuke before another more ominous crisis developed. On August 2, 1990 Saddam Husain invaded the tiny country of Kuwait at the head of the Persian Gulf on Iraq's northern border. Angry that Kuwait had refused to cancel Iraqi debts accumulated during the Iran-Iraq War, Saddam accused the wealthy emirate of driving down oil prices through over-production, and of slant drilling into Iraqi oilfields. The 100,000 man Iraqi invasion force, a small part of his army of half a million, posed an immediate threat to Saudi Arabia. The tiny Saudi army could not possibly defend the kingdom against Iraqi forces within easy striking distance of its oilfields and population centers.

Fresh from what he considered *his* victory over the Soviets, Osama bin Laden offered to defend his country and expel the hated dictator from neighboring Kuwait. He approached the Saudi government boasting that he had 40,000 mujahedeen in Saudi Arabia alone and could raise an army of over 100,000 in three months.[7] Prince Turki recalled that bin Laden "believed that he was capable of preparing an army to challenge Saddam's forces." Turki also noted a disturbing difference in bin Laden. "I saw radical changes in his personality as he changed from a peaceful and gentle man interested in helping Muslims into a person who believed that he would be able to amass and command an army to liberate Kuwait," Turki remembered. "It revealed his arrogance."[8] Given the small numbers and, at best, mediocre performance of the Afghan Arabs in the war against the Soviets and in the struggle to overthrow puppet government they left behind after withdrawing, it would have been sheer folly to rely on this band of zealots for any significant military operation. With no formal military training and only limited experience commanding small units in irregular warfare, bin Laden must have been delusional or a religious fanatic to believe he would be taken seriously. The Saudi's wisely called upon their American ally. The U.S. assembled a coalition of half a million troops to expel Saddam from Iraq in less than one hundred hours of ground combat following a lengthy air campaign.

EXILE

Coming on the heels of his disappointment over South Yemen, the Persian Gulf War further disillusioned Osama about his government. Not only had the monarchy dismissed his offer of help out of hand, it had invited the hated Americans onto the sacred soil of Saudi Arabia, where once the feet of the Prophet had trod. Although he had yet to declare the house of Saud unfit to govern Muslims, these events accelerated the process of alienation that would lead him to that fateful step. In the meantime, he decided on voluntary exile. To leave the kingdom, however, he would need to retrieve his passport. According to one account he asked for his passport and exit visa on the pretext of returning to Pakistan to help refugees from the Afghan war.[9] Another story maintains he wanted to mediate among the competing factions in the Afghan civil war.[10] A third source asserts that he journeyed to Pakistan to "liquidate his investments there."[11] This disagreement illustrates just how much mystery surrounds even relatively recent events in bin Laden's life. No doubt believing that with the Yemeni problem solved and the Iraqis removed from Kuwait, bin Laden could do little harm, the government complied with his request. Bin Laden did make the journey to Peshawar, where he found that he no longer controlled the Arab fighters who had remained there. They had been incorporated into Hekmatyar's forces fighting for control of Afghanistan in the vacuum left by Soviet withdrawal.

Bin Laden decided to relocate with his family to Sudan, where Colonel Omar al-Bashir had staged a coup in 1989. Along with Hassan Turabi, al-Bashir turned the country into an authoritarian Islamist state. Before he left Pakistan, however, bin Laden wrapped up his operations there. "Before [Osama] decided to go to Sudan, he decided that everything is finished [in Pakistan]," one of his associates Osama Rushdi explained.

> This is 1992. They sell everything in Peshawar and they said al Qaeda is finished. I have seen that. The Pakistani government [exerted] a lot of pressure against Arab people. So most of the Saudi Arabia people [sic] went to their country. Some of them went to Bosnia. Osama bin Laden didn't order them to go to Bosnia or Chechnya or any other place. He ordered people that can go peacefully back to their country to back, but the problem is for the people who cannot go back to their own country, and bin Laden [felt] some responsibility about those people.[12]

At least some of the Afghan Arabs for whom he felt responsible came with him to Sudan. They would form the nucleus of revived al-Qaeda, although he may initially have wanted little more than to provide them a place to live.

Uncertainty surrounds bin Laden's activities in Sudan and even his reasons for going there. According to Lawrence Wright, the Sudanese government invited him to settle in the country through a letter it sent him in 1990. The Sudanese assured him that he would be welcome in there Islamist state governed by true Sharia and offered the added enticement of lucrative construction contracts for the bin Laden Group.[13] No other source corroborates the letter, but the bin Laden Group got a contract to build an airport at Port Said. The family may have sent their wayward brother there in order to kill two birds with one stone. They needed someone to manage the Sudanese projects, and they understood that sending Osama would keep him happy at living in an Islamic state and out of trouble. If that was indeed their aim, they would be sorely disappointed.

Whatever his reasons, bin Laden decided to settle in Khartoum, at least for the time being. He probably sent some of his Afghan followers to Sudan ahead of him to rent farms and houses.[14] He moved to the Sudanese capital with his four wives and many children, opened an office there, and bought a farm outside the city. Was he looking for a new base from which to prepare and eventually launch more jihad operations, as some analysts believe or simply seeking to start over in a land ruled according to the teachings of the Prophet as others have proposed?

Whatever his original intent, the Saudi millionaire soon heard the call to jihad once again. The social environment of his new home facilitated his radical activities. In the early 1990s, Sudan provided a safe haven for Islamist extremists from groups throughout the Arab world.[15] His later notoriety makes it easy to forget that in the 1990s he was but one of many jihadist leaders in the Arab world. The U.S. focus on bin Laden and al-Qaeda has blinded Americans to the extent and depth the radical element in what scholars call the "Islamic Awakening" or the "New Islamic Discourse".[16] This movement seeks an Islamic solution to the challenge of modernity, a solution which does not involve westernization. Islamists wish to embrace the technological and other advantages of the West without accepting the values of the culture that produced them. Because this ideological movement began as a challenge to the belief that secular nationalism provided the best way to modernize, Islamists met with repression, especially in Egypt. Repression in turn bred extremism. Denied legitimate avenues of political participation, they turned to violence. The 1970s and 1980s saw a proliferation of extremist groups throughout the Muslim world, many of them developing within the Middle East. While only a small percentage of Islamists advocated violence, those that did demonstrated a willingness to use force indiscriminately against men, women, and children in attacks designed to cause mass casualties. Collectively as well as individually, these Islamist extremists posed a serious threat to their own governments and the Western nations that supported them.

Sudan's willingness to host so many of members of extremist organizations created an opportunity for them to cooperate with one another and to create networks that have persisted to the present. In 1991, Turabi hosted a conference of Islamists from around the world, many of them members of the most violent Islamist groups. Bin Laden attended but was neither an organizer nor a central figure at the meeting.[17] However, either at the conference or in its aftermath, Osama re-engaged with some of his allies, particularly the Egyptian medical doctor Ayman al-Zawahiri. Zawahiri's al-Jihad group had broken with the Muslim Brotherhood over the use of violence. He had treated refugees in Afghanistan and been involved with the creation of al-Qaeda, though his organization remained separate. Sometime during bin Laden's stay in Sudan the two groups merged.

AYMAN AL-ZAWAHIRI

The relationship between bin Laden and Zawihiri is complex and ambiguous. The Egyptian has been content to remain the number two man in al-Qaeda, but many analysts consider him the brains of the operation. Perhaps he understood that given bin Laden's ego, it was wiser to the let the Saudi be the titular leader and public face of the movement. One author insists that "it was bin Laden's vision to create an international jihad corps," and that without him Zawihiri and his followers would have remained preoccupied with overthrowing the government of Europe.[18] Former CIA analyst Bruce Riedel insists that it was the other way around: Zawihiri had the global vision bin Laden lacked.[19] Riedel's argument is far more plausible. Zawihiri was far better educated and more widely traveled than bin Laden. He is also probably smarter. Osama has never shown signs of sweeping original thought. Despite his religious fanaticism, he has always seemed to be deeply impressionable. If his wealth and standing in the Arab world had not made him so much more valuable alive, he is exactly the sort of man who would have been recruited in his youth as suicide bomber.

Because of his important role in al-Qaeda and his influence on Osama bin Laden, Zawahiri's merit careful consideration. After the 9/11 attacks he produced a length treatise detailing his theology and strategy for global jihad. Zawahiri divided the world as two armed camps.

"This point in Islamic history is witness to a furious struggle between the powers of the infidels, tyrants, and haughtiness, on the one hand, and the Islamic *uma* and its *mujahid* vanguard on the other," he declared.[20] He forbad befriending the infidels and preached undying hatred of them. He also preached the need for jihad against pro-Western rulers of Muslim countries. "One of the greatest and most individually binding jihads in this day and age is *jihad* waged against those apostate rulers who reign over Islamic lands and govern without sharia—the friends of Jews and Christians," he proclaimed.[21]

Zawahiri also opposed popular democracy as un-Islamic. "Know that democracy, that is the 'rule of the people,' is a new religion that defies the masses by giving them right to legislate without being shackled down to any other authority," he wrote.[22] The other authority to which he referred was *sharia* as interpreted by the *ulema.* "The bottom line regarding democracies is that the right to make laws is given to someone other than Allah Most High," he reasoned. "So whoever is agreed to this is an infidel—for he has taken gods in place of Allah."[23]

Like most revolutionaries, Zawahiri could justify any excess in the name of his righteous cause. Killing the innocent, even other Muslims, in order to kill the enemy was permissible because "the tyrants and enemies of Allah always see to it that their organizations and military escorts are set among the people and populace, making it difficult to hunt them down in isolation," he explained.[24] He also justified deceit against the infidels. "Deception in warfare requires that the *mujahid* and wait for an opportunity against his enemy, while avoiding confrontation at all possible costs," he counseled. "For triumph in almost every case is [achieved] through deception."[25] Like most religious fanatics, Zawahiri could use legalistic argument to justify anything. Finally, Zawahiri extolled martyrdom above all else. "The best of people, then, are those who are prepared for *jihad* in the path of Allah Most High, requesting martyrdom at any time or place," he concluded.[26]

A DECADE OF TERRORISM

The years Osama bin Laden spent in Sudan witnessed an upsurge in Islamist terrorist activity, but his role in a series of attacks during that time (like so much of his life) remains unclear. In 1993 Ramsey Yousef and Sheik Omar Abdul Rahman (known as "the Blind Sheik") detonated a truck filled with ammonium nitrate in the parking garage beneath the world trade center. The blast killed six people and caused several million dollars in damage. The perpetrators were quickly apprehended. Bin Laden may have funded the Sheik's group, but he does not appear to have been involved in the attack or even known about it ahead of time. In October of that same year, Somali insurgents shot down a Blackhawk helicopter and ambushed an army rangers sent in to rescue the crew, dragging the bodies of dead Americans through the streets of Mogadishu. Bin Laden later praised the operation and claimed Arab Islamists had fought in Somalia. "With Allah's grace," he asserted in a 1997 interview. "Muslims in Somalia cooperated with some Arab Warriors who were in Afghanistan. Together they killed large numbers of American occupation troops."[27] As usual, bin Laden exaggerated the Arab presence and its effect. He did not, however, claim that the Arabs belonged to al-Qaeda or that he personally had had anything to do with the attacks. The Somali fighters have denied that he participated in the operation that downed the helicopter.[28]

Islamist extremist attacks continued throughout the mid 1990s, but bin Laden has not been linked definitively to any of them. In 1995, Saudi terrorists bombed the Saudi National Guard training facility in Riyadh, killing five Americans who worked there. During their trial the four terrorists the Saudi's captured admitted that bin Laden's statements had influenced them. However, Saudi intelligence confided in CIA analyst Bruce Riedel that bin Laden had not been personally involved. The terrorists admissions, however, illustrate that as ideological movement inspiring others to act, al-Qaeda could be just as deadly as when it mounted its own operations. The following year terrorists used a truck bomb to blow up the U.S. military barracks at the Khobar Towers at Dharan Airbase, killing 19 Americans. Once again, bin Laden was initially suspected, and once again (according to Riedel who helped in the investigation), the Saudis determined he had not been involved, although he would later praise the operation.[29] In 1995, Zawahiri's al-Jihad group tried to assassinate Egyptian President Hosni Mubarak in Addis Ababa, Ethiopia. Bin Laden, of course approved, but he does not seem to have been involved.

MAN WITHOUT A COUNTRY

Whatever his original intentions in relocating to Sudan, living there Osama bin Laden's commitment to violent jihad, if it had ever really waned. By early 1994, he had set up new al-Qaeda cells in several countries, including Somalia, Kenya, Yemen, Bosnia, Egypt, Libya, and Tajikistan.[30] His criticism of the Saudi regime also intensified. Osam's family, which had long depended on royal patronage, at first distanced themselves from their wayward brother and then in February 1994 repudiated him. "I myself and all members of the family, whose number exceeds fifty persons, express our strong condemnation and denunciation of all the behavior of Osama, which behavior we do not accept or approve of," Osama's older brother and family patriarch Bakr bin Laden announced.

> As said Osama has been residing outside the Kingdom of Saudi Arabia for more than two years despite our attempts to convince him to return to the right path; we, therefore, consider him to be alone responsible for his statements, actions, and behavior, if truly emanating from him.[31]

The bin Ladens also claimed to have cut Osama off from bin Laden group profits. He was, no doubt, bad for business. Whether they truly turned off the money tap completely is less certain. Bin Laden had spent a small fortune on the Afghan jihad, and, by some accounts, he lost more in Sudan. However, he always seemed to have enough funds to support his large family in Sudan, to relocate them to Afghanistan, and to support them there. He also continued to lead al-Qaeda, which would have been unlikely had all of he been reduced to poverty. When he immigrated to Afghanistan in 1996, he had enough money to shower local sheikhs with gifts. This evidence suggests that whatever they may have said to the contrary, the bin Ladens did not cut off his income completely.

If Osama's own family could no longer ignore his belligerent behavior and inflammatory rhetoric, neither could the Saudi authorities. The same month that Bakr issued his statement, Libyan gunmen fired on bin Laden's house in Khartoum. He blamed the CIA for the attack, but the real culprit behind the it may have been Saudi Intelligence, thought they denied any involvement.[32] In March 1994, Saudi government revoked bin Laden's citizenship. This drastic measure either left Osama unshaken or strengthened his resolve resume the cause of jihad. In December 1994 Osama wrote a scathingly critical letter to Sheik Abdul-Aziz bin Baz, the mufti (leading cleric) of Saudi Arabia. The letter presented a laundry list of complaints against the sheik and, by implication, against the monarchy. Bin Laden accused bin Baz of issuing *fatwas* (religious proclamations) to justify whatever the royal government wanted to do. In particular, he objected to one fatwa calling for peace with the Jews. He singled out for special condemnation the Saudi cleric's willingness to back the regime in support of what he saw as the communist government of Yemen and especially its decision to open the country to "Jewish and Crusader occupation forces [the Americans and their allies]." Perhaps for the first time, bin Laden openly referred to "apostate rulers who wage war on God and his Messenger have neither legitimacy, nor sovereignty over Muslims."[33]

In addition to angering the Saudis, bin Laden attracted the attention of the United States. Although he had as yet conducted no act of terrorism against America or Americans, his connection to so many terrorist groups and professed sympathy for their actions caused concern in Washington. Meanwhile the government of Sudan faced mounting criticism over its open door policy towards extremists. In the spring of 1996 the United Nations Security Council passed a Resolution calling upon the government in Khartoum to desist

> from engaging in activities of assisting, supporting and facilitating terrorist activities and fromgiving shelter and sanctuary to terrorist elements; and henceforth acting in its relations with its neighbours and with others in full conformity with the Charter of the United Nations and with the Charter of the OAU.

The resolution also called upon all member states to reduce their diplomatic interaction with Khartoum.[34] The international pressure had its effect. The Sudanese asked the Saudis to let bin Laden return to the kingdom. The agreed provided he apologized for his inflammatory rhetoric and ceased his extremist activity. Not surprisingly, he refused.

GUEST OF THE TALIBAN

For the second time in a decade, Osama bin Laden was without a home. No country was particularly anxious to take him—with one exception, Afghanistan. After years of civil war the ultra conservative Taliban had captured ninety percent of the country. Their leader Mullah Mohammed Omar held near absolute power, and his religious police unleashed a reign of terror throughout the country, insisting that men wear birds and that women be covered from head to toe in burqas while in public. While these measures exceeded even bin Laden's notion of Muslim purity, he and Omar held common views of jihad and a shared hatred of the West. Osama's still considerable wealth made him a desirable guest, just as it had during the Afghan war against the Soviets. He smoothed his transition into the country and placated Taliban critics with lavish gifts such as new automobiles.[35] This largesse clearly indicates that bin Laden had plenty of money, either from the family's businesses, its individual members, or al-Qaeda sources—probably all three. In May 1996, bin Laden left Sudan with his family and moved into a complex near Kandahar.

Taliban leaders asked him to refrain from the behavior that had gotten him expelled from Sudan. However, much they might agree with him in principle they did not want the repercussions of Western anger any more than had the Sudanese. Mullah Omar and his follows had far more interest in consolidating power in Afghanistan than they did in launching a global jihad. The Saudi, which supported the Taliban, may also have asked them to keep bin Laden quiet. For awhile Osama honored the wishes of his host, but his silence did not last long.

THE FATWA AGAINST JEWS AND CRUSADERS

The years spent in Khartoum with other Islamist radicals had crystallized Osama bin Laden's jihadist worldview. The teachings of the Prophet allowed violence in defense of Islam. Bin Laden understood this teaching as a call to wage war until all of the religion's enemies had been defeated. The apostate regimes of Saudi Arabia and Egypt as well as any other Muslim government that did not implement strict sharia should be attacked and overthrown. Because it supported these regimes, exploited the resources of Muslim countries, and interfered in Muslims affairs in countless other ways, the U.S. must also be attacked. In referring to the American threat, bin Laden used the terms "crusader" and "Zionist-crusader." In his mind (and that of many Islamist extremists) Israel and the U.S. were inexorably linked. He maintained that Zionists dictated American policy toward the Muslim world, and that Israel did America's bidding in the Middle East. Bin Laden's theory of jihad reached its fullest expression in two fatwas, one issued in 1996 and the other in 1998.

The 1996 fatwa, "Declaration of War against the Americans Occupying the Land of the Two Holy Places," detailed a long list of grievances against the West and against what bin Laden now considered a Saudi regime that functioned as an American client. "It should not be hidden from you that the people of Islam had suffered from aggression, iniquity and injustice imposed on them by the Zionist-Crusader alliance and their collaborators," he proclaimed, "to the extent that the Muslims blood became the cheapest and their wealth as loot in the hands of the enemies. Their blood was spilled in Palestine and Iraq." The Iraqi casualties to which bin Laden referred were not those killed in the Gulf War but the many Iraqi civilians, most of them children, who died as a of the U.S. led embargo, which kept medicine and other necessities out of the country. Worst of all, American troops remained on Saudi soil long after the threat from Saddam Husain had receded. Bin Laden called for a boycott of American goods and demanded that U.S. troops leave Saudi Arabia. Fort the first time, he declared the U.S. to the greatest enemy of Islam:

> The regime is fully responsible for what had been incurred by the country and the nation; however the occupying American enemy is the principle and the main cause of the situation. Therefore efforts should be concentrated on destroying, fighting and killing the enemy until, by the Grace of Allah, it is completely defeated.[36]

Both the title and the content of the 1996 fatwa suggest that bin Laden still distinguished between combatants and non-combatants. He called for attacks on U.S. military personnel in Saudi Arabia but fell short of declaring all Americans legitimate targets or even of advocating violence against military personnel outside of Muslim countries. Those restrictions would disappear in his next fatwa, "Jihad against Jews and Crusaders," issued in February 1998. The new fatwa reiterated the complaints of its predecessor, adding to America's crimes the "devastation inflicted on the Iraqi people by the crusader-Zionist alliance, and despite the huge number of those killed, which has exceeded 1 million," another reference to the devastating effects of the blockade. He then issued –

> The ruling to kill the Americans and their allies – civilians and military—is an individual duty for every Muslim who can do it in any country in which it is possible to do it, in order to liberate the al-Aqsa Mosque and the holy mosque [Mecca] from their grip, and in order for their armies to move out of all the lands of Islam, defeated and unable to threaten any Muslim.[37]

In its call to kill any and all Americans where ever and whenever possible, bin Laden's new fatwa deviated from more than one thousand years of Islamic just war theory, which instructed Muslim fighters to distinguish between combatants and non-combatants and to spare women and children.

Bin Laden later explained the logic behind the call for indiscriminate killing of Americans. While Zawahiri argued that women and children would be collateral damage in attacks aimed at military personnel who lived and worked among them, bin Laden justified targeting civilians. "We do not differentiate between those dressed in military uniforms and civilians; they are all targets in this fatwa," he explained.

> American history does not distinguish between civilians and military, not even women and children. They are the ones who used bombs against Nagasaki. Can these bombsdistinguish between infants and military? America does not have a religion that will prevent it from destroying all people.[38]

This bizarre circular reasoning recalled Hitler's justification of the Holocaust. Germany persecuted Jews and engaged in aggressive war, which led to the creation of a powerful anti-German coalition. The Jews were, therefore, to blame for the coalition and must be persecuted further. Bin Laden issued the 1998 Fatwa on behalf of a new organization, the "World Islamic Front." This group may have been a new coalition or merely a new name for al-Qaeda. Whatever the case may be, al-Qaeda continues as the most common name for bin Laden's organization and its affiliates.

Bin Laden's fatwas contradicted Islam's long standing distinction between combatants and non-combatants. After the 9/11 attacks, Osama spoke at some length on this subject. In an October 2001 interview he explained that al-Qaeda killed civilians in retaliation for the civilians he alleged the U.S. killed. "The killing of innocent civilians, as America and some intellectuals claim, is really very strange talk," he concluded.

> When we kill their innocents, the entire world from east to west screams at us. Who said that our blood is not blood, but theirs is? Who made this pronouncement? Who has been getting killed in our countries for decades? More than one million children died in Iraq and others are still dying. Why do we not hear someone screaming or condemning, or even someone's words of consolation or condolence? We kill civilian infidels in exchange for those of our children they kill. This is permissible in law and intellectually.

Not surprisingly, bin Laden fails to say precisely which Islamic law permits such tit-for-tat killing of innocent people. He goes on to explain that since the 9/11 hijackers "did not intend to kill babies" those who died were collateral damage.[39]

In an October 26, 2002 letter to the American people, bin Laden offered an even more convoluted explanation for the murder of civilians. "You may then ask why we are attacking and killing civilians because you have defined them as innocent," he asserted –

> Well this argument contradicts your claim that America is the land of freedom and democracy, where every American irrespective of gender, color, age or intellectual ability has a vote. It is a fundamental principle of any democracy that the people choose their leaders, and as such, approve and are party to the actions of their elected leaders. So 'In the land of freedom' each American is

> 'free' to select their leader because they have the right to do so, and as such they give consent to the policies their elected Government adopts. This includes the support of Israel manifesting itself in many ways including billions of dollars in military aid. By electing these leaders, the American people have given their consent to the incarceration of the Palestinian people, the demolition of Palestinian homes and the slaughter of the children of Iraq.[40]

Since America was a popular democracy, all of its citizens shared responsibility for their government's actions. According to this perverse logic, there was no such thing as an American non-combatant. He failed to explain how the children who died on 9/11 fell under the same death sentence as their parents. Nor did he consider six million loyal Muslim American citizens.

AL-QAEDA ATTACKS

Despite his increasingly inflammatory rhetoric, bin Laden had yet to actually attack the U.S. or its citizens. At the time of his 1998 fatwa plans were already afoot to turn words into deeds. On August 7, 1998, terrorists launched near simultaneous attacks on the US embassies in Nairobi, Kenya and Darussalam, Tanzania. The Nairobi embassy bombing killed 291 people, most of them Kenyans, and injured 5000. The Darussalam embassy attack killed 10 and injured 77.[41] Despite efforts to deny involvement, Osama could not escape blame for the devastating attacks. One of the Tanzanian terrorists was capture and revealed under interrogation that al-Qaeda had planned and conducted the operation.

On the bases of this and other evidence, the Clinton administration decided that it must act decisively against the terrorist organization. The US launched cruise missiles at al-Qaeda training camps in Afghanistan and a pharmaceutical factory in Sudan. The camp attacks killed few and did little permanent damage. The attack on the factory was based on faulty intelligence that it was a dual-use facility manufacturing chemicals for use in weapons as well as medicine. The embassy attacks did, temporarily at least, heighten U.S. awareness of the terrorist threat. As a result, customs and law enforcement did manage to foil a plot to attack targets in the U.S. during the millennium celebrations on News Eve 1999/2000, including a plan to bomb Los Angeles' International Airport. This successful interdiction may have led to overconfidence about the security of U.S. borders.

On 12 October 2000, al-Qaeda struck again, this time against a military target. As the destroyer USS Cole lay at anchor in Aden harbor, Yemen, where it had stopped to refuel, suicide bombers piloted a small boat loaded with explosives up to the ship and detonated it. The attack killed 19 sailors and wounded several others. Only skillful damage control by its captain kept the vessel afloat. These overseas did not produce the alarm they should have. Americans had grown used to attacks on military forces overseas incidents, which had been occurring since the 1983 Marine barracks bombing in Beirut, Lebanon. The state department further hardened its embassies, but few in government took the threat of an attack on the American homeland very seriously. As an indication of this complacency, airlines rigorously screened passengers and baggage on foreign flights but were noticeably lax on domestic ones.

MYTHIC HERO

The success of al-Qaeda operations and America's ability to respond to them effectively emboldened Osama and increased his stature in the Muslim world. Some of his closest associates attest to the U.S. role in strengthening the bin Laden myth. "Do you know what made him famous?," one Guantanamo Bay detainee asked rhetorically. "I will tell you: America. By the media and television and by magazines. Everybody is talking about Osama bin Laden."[42] The head of a Peshawar madrasa that had graduate members of the Taliban corroborated this conclusion:

> I think America has made Osama a supernatural being. Wherever the terrorism occurs, right away they think of him. I don't think he has such influence, or such control and resources. Osama bin Laden has become a symbol for the whole Islamic world. All those outside powers who are trying to crush Muslims interfering with them. Yes, he is a hero to us, but it is America itself who first made him a hero.[43]

This statement indicates that bin Laden was on the way to achieving one of his major goals. He wished to portray America's war against him and al-Qaeda into a war against Islam.

9/11

The events of September 11, 2001 have been etched into the memory of every American alive at the time. The planning and execution of the attacks have been exhaustively studied by the 9/11 Commission and a host of academic and popular works. While much information remains classified and more remains to be discovered, the event itself is fairly well understood. Bin Laden and his associates had been planning the operation for several years and had smuggled in the terrorists as much as a year prior to the attack. The morning of the attack 19 hijackers boarded four aircraft. They flew two into the twin towers of the World Trade Center and a third into the Pentagon. Courageous passengers prevented the fourth flying missile from being delivered to its target, forcing the hijackers to crash plane into a Pennsylvania field.

As with previous al-Qaeda operations, the idea for the 9/11 attacks does not seem to have originated with Osama bin Laden. The *Report of the 9/11 Commission* credits the Egyptian Khalid Sheikh Mohammed (KSM) with proposing and developing the plan. He had first intended to blow up a number of planes departing Manila airport over the Pacific in 1994, but authorities foiled that plot. In 1996 he met bin Laden in Afghanistan.

> KSM briefed [Mohammed Atef-9/11 hijackers] and bin Laden on the first World Trade Center bombing, the Manilla air plot, the cargo carriers plan, and other activities pursued by KSM and his colleagues in the Philippines. KSM also presented a proposal that would involve training pilots would crash planes into buildings in the United States. This proposal eventually become the 9/11 plot.[44]

The conclusion that KSM masterminded the 9/11 plot corroborates a considerable body of evidence indicating that bin Laden has never been the brains of al-Qaeda. Al Jazeera chief investigative reporter Yosri Fourda offered a poignant assessment of bin-Laden's abilities and his role in al-Qaeda. "It doesn't surprise me [that Khalid Sheikh Mohammed organized 9/11]," Fourda observed.

> It's not exactly bin Laden's territory. He's not very fond of details, looking at details. He's the enigma; he's the chairman of the company, so to speak. He is the symbol of the organization. He is the symbol of the organization. He would still need people like Khaled Sheikh Mohammed to be advising him on certain operations, and Khalid Sheikh Mohammed would, in turn, need people to execute things.[45]

AFTERMATH

Operationally, the 9/11 attacks were brilliantly planned and almost flawlessly executed. They struck economic and military targets of great strategic and symbolic importance, achieving the dramatic effect all terrorists seek. Estimates place the number of viewers who saw video footage of the attacks at one billion. 9/11also represented the culmination of Osama bin Laden's jihadist journey. He had begun as pious young man who had been swayed by Islamist teaching in school. Azzam recruited him to the cause of jihad during the Afghan War against the Soviets. He returned a hero, only to be rebuffed by his own country following the Iraqi invasion of Kuwait. The Saudis turned to the U.S. for defense against Saddam Hussein rather than accept bin Laden's offer to raise a force of mujahedeen fighters to defend the kingdom. After the war he went into voluntary exile, first in Sudan and then in Afghanistan. During that exile he came to believe that jihad must be waged against apostate Muslim regimes as well as the United States, which backed them. The U.S. response to 9/11 would change his fortunes but not end his campaign of terror. Nothing could dampen his ardor for aggressive jihad.

NOTES

1. Osama Rushdi, quoted in Peter Bergen, *The Osama bin Laden I Know* (New York: Free Press, 2006), p. 106.
2. Lawrence Wright, *The Looming Tower: Al-Qaeda and the Road to 9/11* (New York: Alfred Knopf, 2006), p. 151.
3. Abu Walid al Misiri, in Bergen, *Osama bin Laden I Knew,* p. 109.

4. Turki and Clarke quoted in Steve Cole, *The Bin Ladens: An Arabian Family in the American Century* (New York: Penguin, 2008), p. 46.
5. Bruce Riedel, *The Search for al-Qaeda: Its Leadership, Ideology, and Future* (Washington, DC: Brookings Institute Press, 2008), p. 47.
6. Ibid.
7. Abu Jandal, Osama bin Laden's body guard, in ibid., p. 112.
8. Prince Turki in ibid., p. 112.
9. Ibid., p. 49.
10. Wright, *Looming Tower*, p. 161.
11. Coll, *Bin Ladens*, p. 381.
12. Osama Rusdi in ibid., p. 106.
13. Wright, *Looming Tower*, p. 164.
14. Coll, *Bin Ladens*, p. 381.
15. Riedel, *Search for al-Qaeda*, p. 49.
16. Sherifa Zuhur, *A Hundred Osamas: Islamist Threats and the Future of Counterinsurgency* (Carlisle Barracks, PA: Strategic Studies Institute, 2005), pp. 19-23.
17. Riedel, *Search for al-Qaeda*, p. 49.
18. Wright, *Looming Tower*, p. 332.
19. Riedel, *Search for al-Qaeda*, p. 16.
20. Ayman al-Zawahiri, in Raymond Ibrahim, *The Al Qaeda Reader* (New York: Broadway Books, 2007), p. 70.
21. Ibid., p. 94.
22. Ibid., p. 130.
23. Ibid., p. 133.
24. Ibid., p. 169.
25. Ibid., p. 142.
26. Ibid., pp. 145-146.
27. Quoted in John Esposito, *Unholy War: Terror in the Name of Islam* (Oxford, UK: Oxford University Press, 2002), p. 22.
28. Riedel, *Search for al-Qaeda*, p. 51.
29. Ibid., p. 51.
30. Coll, *Bin Ladens*, p. 409.
31. Bakr bin Laden, quoted in ibid., p. 408.
32. Riedel, *Search for al-Qaeda*, p. 54.
33. Osama bin Laden, "Open Letter to Sheik Abdul-Aziz bin Baz on the Invalidity of his Fatwa on Peace with the Jews," translated by the Counter Terrorism Center, U.S. Military Academy, West Point, available at http://en.wikisource.org/wiki/Open_Letter_to_Shaykh_Bin_Baz_on_the_Invalidity_of_his_Fatwa_on_Peace_with_the_Jews, accessed May 31, 2009.

34. UN Security Council Document, S/RES/1054 (1996), 26 April 1996, available at http://daccessdds.un.org/doc/UNDOC/GEN/N96/107/86/PDF/N9610786.pdf?OpenElement, accessed May 31, 2009.
35. Account of Vahid Mojdeh, who held various posts in the Afghan government, in Bergen, *Osama bin Laden I Knew*, p. 164.
36. Osama bin Laden, "Declaration of War against the Americans Occupying the Land of the Two Holy Places," in *Al Quds Al Arabi* [news paper published in London], August 1996, available at http://www.pbs.org/newshour/terrorism/international/fatwa_1996.html, accessed June 1, 2009.
37. Osama bin Laden, "Jihad against Jews and Crusaders," February 23, 1998, http://www.fas.org/irp/world/para/docs/980223-fatwa.htm, accessed June 1, 2009.
38. *Esquire* interview with Osama bin Laden, February 1999, in *Compilation of Osama bin Laden Statements, 1994-January 2004* (Washington, DC: FBIS, 2004), p. 99, available at http://www.fas.org/irp/world/para/ubl-fbis.pdf, accessed June 1, 2009.
39. Osama bin Laden, Al Jazeera interview, October 2001, aired by CNN, February 5, 2002, available at http://archives.cnn.com/2002/WORLD/asiapcf/south/02/05/binladen.transcript/index.html, accessed August 1, 2009.
40. Osama bin Laden, Letter to the American People, in *Compilation of Osama bin Laden Statements*, p. 216.
41. Ibid.
42. Unidentified detainee, quoted in Bergen, *Osama bin Laden I Knew*, p. 227.
43. Darul Ulon Haqqani, quoted in ibid., p. 227.
44. *The Report of the 9/11 Commission* (Washington, DC: Government Printing Office, 2004), p. 149, available at http://www.9-11commission.gov/report/911Report.pdf, accessed June 17, 2009
45. Yosri Fouda, in Bergen, *Bin Laden I Knew*, p. 303.

Chapter 6

BIN LADEN AND AL-QAEDA, POST-9/11

APPRAISING 9/11

Osama bin Laden was initially elated by his successful attacks on New York and Washington. Operationally, the strikes had succeeded his expectations. True, the fourth airplane never made it to its target, which may have been the White House or the Capital Building, but the collapse of the Twin Towers had more than compensated for that failure. With all his experience in the family construction business, bin Laden had not expected the Towers to collapse. The intense heat of the fire destroyed the steel skeleton and the weight of the building above the impact point brought them toppling down on the floors below bringing the entire structure to the ground in a pancake effect. Devastating as the attack had been, it could have been much worse. Casualties proved unexpectedly light. The hijackers had attacked a bit too early in the day. New Yorkers characteristically come to work later and work later than people in other cities, so the Towers had not been full. More importantly, the city and the occupants of the Towers had learned from the 1993 bombings how to evacuate quickly and efficiently. Most of the people who worked on the floors below the impact point of the airplanes got out before the buildings collapsed.

Bin Laden later reflected on how much the attacks had accomplished. "I was thinking that the fire from the gas in the plane would melt the iron structure of the building and collapse the area where the plane hit and all the floors above it only. This is all we hoped for," he told a Saudi supporter in late 2001. On the day of the attack, he had told his gleeful followers who cheered as they watched the first plane hit the south tower to "be patient." More attacks would unfold in the next hour and a half.[1] Another follower raced to tell bin Laden what he had seen of the attacks on television. Osama responded with a hand gesture meaning, "I know, I know."[2]

Despite indisputable evidence of his involvement, Osama initially denied responsibility for the attacks as he had with the East Africa embassy bombings. Unlike most terrorist organizations, which eagerly claim responsibility for their operations, al-Qaeda preferred to keep its enemies guessing. "I have already said that I am not involved in the 11 September attacks in the United States," bin Laden told a correspondent in Pakistan on September 28, 2001.

> As a Muslim, I try my best to avoid telling a lie. Neither I had any knowledge of these attacks nor do I consider the killing of innocent women, children, and other humans as an appreciable act. Islam strictly forbids causing harm to innocent women, children, and other people. Such a practice is forbidden ever in the course of a battle.[3]

Bin Laden could tell such a lie with a straight face and clean conscience because radical clerics had issued fatwas allowing deception of Islam's enemies.

Deny responsibility for the attacks though they might in the immediate aftermath of 9/11, al-Qaeda's leaders did not maintain their denials once the U.S. air campaign against Afghanistan began. In April 2002, al-Jazirah television aired excerpts from an al-Qaeda tape in which bin Laden and his second-in-command, Ayman al-Zawahiri voiced their true feelings about the operation. "This great victory, which was achieved, is due, in fact, to the grace of Allah alone," Zawahiri proclaimed.

> It was not due to our skillfulness or superiority, but it is due to Allah's blessing alone. Allah Almighty grants his mercy to whoever He wants. Allah looks into the hearts of his slaves and chooses from them those who are qualified to win His grace, mercy, and blessings. Those 19 brothers, who left [their homes], made efforts, and offered their lives for Allah's cause—Allah has favored them with this conquest, which we are enjoying now.[4]

For his part, bin Laden promised more attacks and linked them to his favorite grievances against the U.S., in particular the plight of Palestinians and the presence of American forces in Saudi Arabia. "The United States will not even dream of enjoying security if we do not experience security as a living reality in Palestine, the land of the two holy mosques, and all Muslim countries," he declared.[5]

OPERATION ENDURING FREEDOM

Gleeful though he was about the destruction, loss of life, and economic impact of his attacks on New York and Washington, bin Laden had not launched airplanes into buildings just to achieve those immediate results. More than anything else he wished to draw U.S. forces into a protracted war. He had studied the American failure in Vietnam and personally contributed to the Soviet defeat in Afghanistan. He had also seen how quickly President Clinton withdrew U.S. forces from Somalia after the death of Army Rangers in Mogadishu. Perhaps he also recalled America's precipitous withdrawal from Lebanon following the bombing of the Marine barracks in Beirut in 1983. Bin Laden had approved the 9/11talks for the expressed purpose of provoking the U.S. into invading Afghanistan. History suggested that al-Qaeda could sap American strength in an unconventional war in which Islamist insurgents would wear down the U.S. military as the Viet Cong had done in Southeast Asia and the mujahedeen had done to the Soviets in Afghanistan.

In April 2001, bin Laden confided to his future Pakistani biographer this ulterior motive behind the 9/11 attacks. According to Hamid Mir, bin Laden told him that as a result of the attacks, the U.S. would invade Afghanistan, the Taliban would fall, and al-Qaeda would wage jihad against the occupying American force as it had against the Soviets.[6] Sayf Adel, an al-Qaeda military commander, explained this strategy in greater depth. "Our ultimate objective of these painful strikes against the head of the serpent was to prompt it to come out of its hole," Adel declared.

> This would make it easier for us to deal consecutive blows to undermine it and tear it apart. It would foster our credibility in front of our nation and the beleaguered people of the world. A person will react randomly when he receives painful strike on the top of his head from an undisclosed enemy. Such strikes will force the person to carry out random acts and provoke him to make serious and sometimes fatal mistakes. This was what actually happened. The first reaction was the invasion of Afghanistan and the second was invasion of Iraq.[7]

Although the strategy provoked the desired response, the invasion of Afghanistan did not unfold as bin Laden had hoped. The U.S. military had learned from its own experience in Vietnam and decided that a large scale operation with U.S. ground forces was neither feasible nor desirable. The Pentagon also had no plan for a full-scale conventional invasion. It had to improvise. Washington decided to exploit the civil war that had been raging since the Soviets had left Afghanistan. U.S. Special Operations Command and the CIA deployed small teams of operatives to support the Northern Alliance of Tadjik and Turcoman tribes, which had been fighting the Pashtun Taliban and its al-Qaeda allies. The Northern Alliance controlled only ten percent of Afghanistan, but its territory was adjacent to former Soviet central Asian republics. Eager for a free hand against Chechen rebels, Russian President Vladimir Putin supported the U.S. leasing of old Soviet air bases in Uzbekistan and Kyrgyzstan. These bases became staging areas for American operations within Afghanistan.

Direct support combined with military supplies and funding turned the tide of the war. Northern Alliance forces provided with close air support rolled back the Taliban in a matter of weeks. The war combined the tactics of the thirteenth-century with those of the 21. Special Forces teams called in airstrikes using laptops with satellite communications, and Northern Alliance forces followed up on bombings with cavalry charges to finish off the shell-shocked Taliban. Afghan forces did most of the fighting against the Taliban and suffered most of the casualties. The widespread unpopularity of the Taliban also contributed to its rapid collapse. A former Taliban Foreign Ministry official who wrote a book on the Taliban noted that because the group never enjoyed popular support and ruled through brutality and terror, it feared revenge from the Afghan populace.[8] Television cameraman Peter Jouvenal described the mood in Kabul after the city fell to the Northern Alliance. "The people were overjoyed to be relieved of such a suppressive regime," he concluded.[9]

Even so, the speed of the Taliban collapse shocked its supporters and opponents alike. "No one believed the country would fall so quickly," a Kuwaiti captured during the fighting told American interrogators. Osama bin Laden narrowly escaped capture. He responded to Operation Enduring Freedom by threatening more attacks on the U.S. The day the American bombing campaign against the Taliban began, he appeared on television in a video tape that may have been made some time earlier. "To America, I say only a few words to it and its people," he proclaimed. "I swear by God, who has elevated the skies without pillars, neither America nor the people who live in it will dream of security before we live it in Palestine, and not before all the infidel armies leave the land of Muhammad, peace be upon him."[10]

Although Bin Laden did not get his war of attrition, he did, however, disappoint his pursuers. He escaped from Kandahar to the rugged Tora Bora region along the Pakistan border, terrain he knew well from the time he had spent there during the 1980s. U.S. forces could not easily reach this remote area, and its many caves provided protection from American air strikes. If necessary, he and his forces could slip over the Pakistan border in the country's remote and largely ungoverned Federally Administered Tribal Area. An operation in December failed to capture bin Laden or destroy al-Qaeda and the Taliban. Operation Anaconda launched the following March inflicted heavy casualties on insurgent forces in the Shahi-Kot Valley and Ama Mountains, but once again bin Laden and Mullah Omar escaped.

The failure of the Tora Bora operation came under criticism at the time and will be the subject of discussion by military analysts for years to come. *Army Times* reporter Sean Naylor argues that the decision not to deploy heavy artillery to the valley floor contributed significantly to the failure.[11] Reliance upon local forces that may have been unwilling to pursue the fugitives was probably also a factor. In a land where revenge has been the law of the land for centuries and blood-feuds can last decades, few Afghans wanted to make enemies of al-Qaeda or the Taliban, especially since they could not be sure how long the Americans would stay to protect them. "America's special forces are very good, but the mistake they made [at Tora Bora] was they relied on Afghans for information," concluded cameraman and former British army officer Peter Jouvenal. "And so it was pretty easy for Osama to slip out. It's no criticism of the Special Forces. I think there weren't enough of them on the ground."[12] A local Afghan militia leader who fought in the battle identified yet another tactical failure: "My personal view is if the Americans had blocked the way out to Pakistan, al-Qaeda would not have had a way to escape."[13]

Despite the disappointment of bin Laden's escape, the rapid conquest of Afghanistan offered the U.S. and its allies a golden opportunity to reduce the Taliban to a localized, containable threat, and perhaps destroy al-Qaeda central as an effective organization. However, the Bush administration wasted the opportunity. Considering major combat operations at an end, it handed responsibility over to NATO's International Security Assistance Force (ISAF), a collection of forces from more than twenty nations, few of whom had the resources, training, or stomach for a protracted fight. The U.S. also provided very little development money to the impoverished country. Seeing an opportunity to remove Saddam Hussein under the guise of the "Global War on Terrorism" (GWOT), President Bush and his advisors, especially Secretary of Defense Donald Rumsfeld and Vice-President Dick Cheney, wanted to concentrate troops in the Persian Gulf for the invasion of Iraq. The decision to begin a new war before the old one had been finished would cost America dearly. Taking the pressure off al-Qaeda and the Taliban allowed them much needed breathing room in which to regroup. They would wage an insurgent campaign that would grow more intense over the next eight years.

GLOBAL JIHAD

While Al-Qaeda "central" spent the next several years regrouping in Pakistan, its global network of cells and affiliate organizations continued to wage a campaign of terror against the West. According to former CIA analyst Bruce Riedel, al-Qaeda has pursued a three-pronged strategy since 9/11: tie down U.S. forces in wars of attrition (Afghanistan and Iraq); consolidate its base in South Asia; and establish "franchises" around the Muslim world. These franchises would continue to attack apostate regimes and Western countries, perhaps baiting them into more quagmire wars.[14] These attacks might also produce a strong backlash against Muslim communities in Western countries, thus increasing support for the global jihad and confirming bin Laden's claim that the real target of the U.S. and its allies was not al-Qaeda but Islam itself.

The specter of another 9/11 would haunt the U.S. for years to come. As devastating as the attacks were, they forced the West and its allies to consider an even more frightening scenario. Unlike past terrorist and insurgent organizations, al-Qaeda would use a weapon of mass destruction (WMD) if it could acquire one. Weapons of Mass Destruction included chemical agents, germs, and nuclear bombs or radioactive material. Chemical agents were first used in battle during World War I. Poisoned gas caused much suffering but accomplished little else. Chemical weapons have limited use unless the enemy can be trapped in a confined space. The only major terrorist attack with a chemical weapon occurred in 1995, when the Japanese terrorist cult Aum Shinrikyo released Sarin gas in the Tokyo subway. The attack killed 54 and injured hundreds of others. Biological agents are potentially much more lethal but far more dangerous to use. Terrorist who decided employ them would risk the infection spreading to their own country. Only anthrax kills in a controlled manner without serious risk of such a back lash. An anthrax attack immediately after 9/11 turned out to be home grown and largely ineffective. Nuclear weapons present the greatest threat. During the Cold War the Soviet Union developed suitcase-size nuclear bombs capable of destroying the heart of a city. A conventional warhead could also be smuggled into the country in a shipping container. Another alternative would be to build a "dirty bomb," radioactive material dispersed over a wide area by a conventional explosion, rendering the area uninhabitable for years. Bin Laden made his interest in WMD clear as early as 1999. "Acquiring nuclear and chemical weapons is a religious duty," he proclaimed.[15] So far, it seems, he has not been able to fulfill that duty.

AL-QAEDA'S BOMBING CAMPAIGN

Attractive as WMD may be, however, difficulty acquiring and using it has confined al-Qaeda to conventional bombs. This weapon has proved deadly enough. In the four years following 9/11, al-Qaeda cells and affiliates would strike from Asia to Europe. For each successful attack, Western security agencies would foil dozens of other. The attacks themselves and the cost of preventing others like them would run to billions of dollars and change, perhaps irrevocably, how millions of people would live their lives on a day to day basis.

The world did not have long to wait in learning that al-Qaeda was alive and well. On October 12, 2002, terrorists from Indonesian based *Jemaah Islamiya*, an Islamist terrorist organization linked to al-Qaeda, bombed a nightclub in the small wealthy, South Asian kingdom of Bali. The attack killed 202 people and wounded over 100 others. Australian tourists comprised the largest number of those killed. Bin Laden was quick to praise the attack and remind the world of its motivation. "We warned Australia before not to join in [the war] in Afghanistan, and [against] its despicable effort to separate East Timor," Osama proclaimed in a taped message aired on Al Jazeerah television, November 12, 2002. "It ignored the warning until it woke up to the sounds of explosions in Bali."[16]

A wave of al-Qaeda sponsored attacks ensued. During the same month as the Bali bombings and throughout the following year, Russia suffered from a series of terrorist attacks. Though perpetrated by Chechen separatists, these bombings probably enjoyed al-Qaeda support and perhaps direct assistance. In November 2003, al-Qaeda carried out two deadly bomb attacks against targets in Istanbul, Turkey. On November 15, they detonated truck bombs at two synagogues, and on November 20, two more bombs rocked the HSBC bank and the British consulate. The attacks killed 57 civilians and wounded over 700. On November 16, bin Laden sent a statement to al Jazeerah television claiming responsibility for the synagogue bombings, which the Martyr Abu-Hafs al-Misri

Brigades, affiliated with al-Qaeda carried out because, he said, Israeli intelligence operated out of the building.[17]

If the incidents in Bali, Moscow, and Istanbul seemed far removed from the centers of Western power, the next attacks would occur much closer to home. On March 11, 2004, the Abu Hafs al-Masri Brigade detonated a series of bombs on commuter trains and in a terminal in Madrid Spain, killing 191 people and wounding over 600 others. Spanish police cornered the terrorist group in an apartment as it was preparing to carry out a second attack. The cornered terrorists committed suicide by detonating their explosives. The group affiliated with al-Qaeda claimed it carried out the attacks to punish Spain for its participation in the American-led invasion of Iraq.[18] They planned their operation to coincide with Spanish elections. Unfortunately, Spanish voters did what al-Qaeda wanted but not because of the Madrid bombings. They voted Prime Minister Azner out of office, and his successor withdrew the Spanish contingent from the Iraq war coalition. Spaniards had never favored the deployment in the first place.

A month after the Madrid bombings bin Laden issued an offer of peace to the Europeans in which he explained the rational for the attacks. "There is a lesson [to be learned] regarding what happens in occupied Palestine and what happened on September 11 and March 11," he lectured. "Our actions are merely reactions to yours—represented by the murder and destruction of our people in Afghanistan, Iraq, and Palestine."[19] When Spain announced that it would withdraw its troops from Iraq, al-Qaeda announced that the country would no longer be targeted. The terrorists appeared to have won another substantial victory.

A year after the Madrid attacks, Britain came into the terrorists' crosshairs. An al-Qaeda cell in the United Kingdom carried out a sophisticated attack on the London transit system. On July 7, 2005, three suicide bombers detonated backpack bombs on three different trains in the London Underground during rush hour. A fourth terrorist detonated his bomb on a bus in Tavistock Square after discovering the Underground station he was supposed to have entered had been closed for repairs. The attack killed 52 people and injured more than 770. Three of the four terrorists had been born in the British Isles and the fourth had emigrated there with his parents as an infant. Two of the bombers had traveled to Pakistan in November 2004 and February 2005, where they probably received support and instructions from al-Qaeda members.[20] On July 21 another terrorist cell launched four more attacks on London Underground trains. This time, however, their bombs failed to detonate, and all the terrorists along with their support cell were arrested. Although they denied any relationship to the July 7 bombers, most analysts agree that al-Qaeda intended the operations to be linked.

Bin Laden's second-in-command Ayman al-Zawahiri praised the attackers and chastised the United Kingdom for supporting the U.S. in Iraq and Afghanistan. "The blessed raid that, like its illustrious predecessors in New York [9/11], and Madrid [3/11], took the battle to the enemy's own soil," he declared.

> After long centuries of his taking the battle to our soil and after his hordes and armed forces occupied our lands in Chechnya, Afghanistan, Iraq, and Palestine, and after centuries of his occupying out land while enjoying security at home. This blessed raid, like its illustrious predecessors, came to pass thanks to the racing of the vanguards of Islam to achieve martyrdom in defense of their religion and sanctities and security.[21]

These major incidents represent the most serious in a steady stream of al-Qaeda attacks following 9/11. At the time they occurred, each provoked considerable debate over who had instigated them. Despite much talk of "leaderless resistance," considerable evidence suggests that al-Qaeda central decided which operations would be launched and approximately when they should be carried out. Even after the disruption caused by the invasion of Afghanistan, al-Qaeda remained a formidable terrorist. At the same time that maintained strategic direction over operations, however, it left much of their planning and execution to local cells and affiliates. Dubbed "centralization of decision making and decentralization of execution," this management style proved highly effective.[22] As America and its allies applied relentless pressure on bin Laden and the other leaders, they could no longer easily move resources around the world as they had done for the East Africa embassy bombings. They had to rely on local talent. However, much of this talent had been pre-positioned during the 1990s as the thousands of young men who had passed through al-Qaeda training camps returned home to await further instructions. The dramatic success of 9/11 coupled with the efforts of these al-Qaeda training camp graduates facilitated recruitment of new terrorists. The leader of the group that had carried out the Madrid train bombings was a former drug dealer who had been radicalized by other Muslims while serving time in Prison. Mohammed Saddique Khan, who led the suicide attack on the London Underground, had been recruited through a youth center at his local Mosque in Leeds.

IRAQ AND AFGHANISTAN

In the eight years since 9/11, the American homeland has not been attacked by al-Qaeda. The cause of this long period of security has been the subject of considerable debate. The Bush administration and its supporters insist that security measures put in place since 9/11 and aggressive interrogation of terrorist suspects (including use of torture) has kept the country safe. Their critics have pointed out that with U.S. servicemen and women dying in Iraq and Afghanistan on a daily basis, al-Qaeda does not need to strike the homeland in order to kill Americans and further the cause of jihad. They also note that the Islamist terrorists have demonstrated great patience, waiting for the right opportunity to strike. Eight years elapsed between the unsuccessful 1993 attack on the World Trade Center and destruction of the Twin Towers.

Security against terrorism has improved in a number of areas since 9/11. Creation of the Department of Homeland Security brought disparate security and disaster management organizations under one roof and improved coordination of their activities. A new Director of National Intelligence and a National Intelligence Center facilitated sharing of information between the FBI and CIA (a serious weakness before 9/11) and among numerous other intelligence agencies. Interrogation of prisoners at the Guantanamo Bay detention facility may have yielded information that foiled terrorist plots, but this contention is difficult to prove since whatever intelligence it garnered remains classified. Any such gains must, of course, be weighed against the adverse international reaction and loss of legitimacy harsh interrogation methods produced.

Open sources do suggest that the U.S. and its allies have enjoyed some success in disrupting al-Qaeda's global operations. The terrorists who bombed the London transit system in July 2005 combined brilliant planning with amateur execution. They carried out their dry run too far in advance of the actual attack and, as a result, did not realize that the Underground station the fourth bomber was supposed to have entered was closed for repairs. They detonated two of their bombs in older "cut and cover" tunnels near the surface, where the space provided by adjacent tracks dissipated the force of the explosions. Twenty-six of the fifty-two fatalities occurred on the one train bombed in a deep tunnel. More careful attention to target selection could have produced far greater loss of life. The failure of the second set of attacks on July 21 occurred because the explosive mixture was too old and had become inert. This mixture of professional and amateur terrorism indicates that al-Qaeda's capacity to move experts around its global network has been diminished. The year before the London bombings, MI5 (Britain's domestic intelligence service) arrested a number of terrorists in an undercover operation dubbed "Crevice." Two of the young men under surveillance during that operation went on to bomb the Underground the following year. MI5 had deemed them too insignificant to operate on their own. The men arrested in March 2004 probably included the masterminds of British al-Qaeda operations. Had they not been caught, the July 2005 attacks would probably have been much worse. MI 5 had made a mistake in letting two of the terrorists fall off its radar, but with some 2000 young British men who had been to Afghanistan to watch, it simply lacked the resources to track everyone.

The United States also enjoyed some dramatic successes, captured a number of terrorist operatives. The most prominent of those apprehended was Khalid Sheikh Mohammed, mastermind of the 9/11 plot. On March 1, 2003, the Pakistani Inter-Services Intelligence Agency in cooperation with the CIA captured Mohammed in Rawalpindi, Pakistan. The United States transported him to its detention facility at the Guantanamo Bay Naval base, where they subjected him to intense interrogation, including water-boarding numerous times. He probably provided some useful intelligence on al-Qaeda, though how much and precisely what remain classified. In February 2008, the Department of Defense charged Mohammed with multiple counts of murder. He allegedly pled guilty in

December 2008, and is awaiting a mental competency hearing before the plea can be accepted.

Improved security, better intelligence sharing, and the capture of al-Qaeda members alone do not, however, explain why the U.S. mainland has not been attacked by al-Qaeda since 9/11. Bin Laden and his associates have repeatedly stated that their expressed purpose in launching the attacks was to provoke a U.S. invasion of Afghanistan. They could not have expected that America would invade Iraq as well, but they certainly welcomed the invasion. Al-Qaeda and its affiliates could concentrate on killing Americans in the occupied countries. At the same time attacks on the U.S. ceased, at least for the time being, they increased dramatically in Western Europe. This pattern of violence suggests that the security of the U.S. homeland during the past eight years stems at least in part from a shift in al-Qaeda strategy. Osama bin Laden would still like to attack the American homeland and would certainly do so given the opportunity, but he seems to be concentrating his efforts on Iraq and Afghanistan and on weakening the resolve of America's European allies by attacking them.

Osama bin Laden has issued a number of statements on the Iraq war. On October 18, 2003, al-Jazeerah television aired his message to the American people. In it he accused the Bush administration of invading Iraq to gain control of the country's oil and to serve the needs of the Zionists. He gloated over the quagmire in which the infidels found themselves and promised devastating consequences for any nation that supported the Americans. The U.S. invasion had was exactly the sort of response to 9/11 he had wanted, a gift from God that allowed him to continue his jihad. "But Allah sent him [Bush] to Baghdad, the seat of the Caliphate, the land of people who prefer death to honey," Osama proclaimed. "They [the Iraqis] turned his profits into losses, his happiness into misery, and now he is merely looking for a way [to go] home." Bin Laden went on to threaten attacks against America's European allies. "We have the right to retaliate at any [given] time and place against [any and] all countries involved—particularly England, Spain, Australia, Poland, Japan, and Italy."[23] Bin Laden proved true to his word. He had already killed Australians in Bali and would bomb the Madrid trains the following March and the London transit system a year later. Following the Madrid bombings, Spain withdrew from the coalition fighting in Iraq. Even though this decision resulted from a change of government rather than intimidation, al-Qaeda claimed victory. Italy too left the coalition following the death of twelve of its soldiers in Iraq.

On the eve of the 2004 presidential election, bin Laden spoke again to the American people. He admonished the them to repudiate the wicked policies of their government and explained al-Qaeda's long-term strategy of attrition. "All we had to do was send two *mujahedeen* to the farthest east to raise aloft a piece of rag with the words 'al-Qaeda' written on it, and the [U.S.] generals came a-scurrying—causing America to suffer human, economic, and political damages while accomplishing nothing worth mentioning aside from providing business [contracts] for their private corporations," he explained.

> On the other hand, we have gained experience in guerrilla and attritional warfare in our jihad against the great and wicked superpower, Russia, which we, along-side the *mujahedeen*, fought for ten years until, bankrupt, it was forced to withdraw [out of Afghanistan in 1989]—all praise be to Allah! And so we are continuing the same policy: to make America bleed till it becomes bankrupt.[24]

Following this message, bin Laden stayed off the airwaves for over a year. Then in January 2006, he released an audiotape in which he offered the American people a truce. If the U.S. would withdraw its forces from Iraq and Afghanistan, al-Qaeda would cease its campaign of terror against America. "The war in Iraq is raging without end [in sight]; the operations in Afghanistan are continually escalating in our favor—praise be to Allah," he stated, reiterating the cost of the war in American blood and treasure. "Pentagon figures show an increase in your casualties and wounded—let alone the massive economic loses, the destruction of soldiers' morale there, and an increase [in cases] of suicide among them."[25] Neither war was going well at the time, but it is hard to believe Osama could have been so deluded as to believe the White House or the public would take his offer seriously. As with most of his pronouncements, the real audience was probably his supporters in the Muslim world. He reminded them periodically of the justness of al-Qaeda's cause and of its inevitable ultimate triumph.

THE AL-QAEDA THREAT

As al-Qaeda has gone deeper underground, gaining precise information on its strength and capabilities has become increasingly difficult. Sources available in the public domain allow only tentative conclusions. Twenty years after its creation and eight years after its most dramatic success, al-Qaeda remains a formidable threat. The central organization seems to have rebuilt itself in the ungoverned border lands between Pakistan and Afghanistan. In cooperation with the Taliban it continues to wage a protracted war to regain control of Afghanistan and threatens the stability of Pakistan. It can still direct operations abroad although it seems the West seems to have diminished its capacity to concentrate resources and talent for dramatic strikes like the East Africa bombings and 9/11.

The election of Democratic President Barack Obama in November 2008 has led to a change in U.S. military strategy. Obama has begun reducing the American presence in Iraq and shifting troops to Pakistan. The U.S. has also put increasing pressure on the new government in Islamabad to take more aggressive action against al-Qaeda and the Taliban operating on its soil. In the spring of 2009, the Pakistani army began an offensive against Taliban forces in the Swat Valley on its Northwest frontier with Afghanistan. In early July, 4000 U.S. Marines in cooperation with Afghan forces launched an offensive to regain control of Helmund Province, while Pakistani blocked escape routes on their side of the border. The offensive was part of Washington's new "clear and hold" strategy, made possible by increasing you use troop strength by more than 20,000.

Gauging the strength of al-Qaeda's global network of cells and affiliates is even more difficult than assessing the capabilities of the central organization. A steady, highly effective, and largely unnoticed campaign supported by U.S. Special Forces has crippled its ability to operate in the Philippines. Islamist extremism in Indonesia also appears to have waned since the days of the Bali bombing. In other areas of the world, however, the al-Qaeda network may have grown stronger. Filled with second-generation young men resentful of their low status and lack of opportunity, the Muslim communities in Western Europe remain a cause of concern.

Many analysts expect the number of terrorist attacks in this region to increase during the next decade. The newspaper, *Die Welt* (the World) reported that intelligence intercept indicate the likelihood of terrorist attacks in Germany on the run-up to its fall elections.[26] If these attacks do materialize, they would be in keeping with al-Qaeda's strategy of pressuring its allies to withdraw from Afghanistan. Non-violent Islamism has grown much stronger in Turkey. As long as this movement experiences success at the ballot box, it may eschew the bomb. However, should the state's historic guardians of secularism, the Turkish military, reassert control as they have in the past, this situation could change dramatically for the worse.

Africa has seen considerable growth in Islamist extremism in recent years. Al-Qaeda in the Maghreb, a terrorist organization affiliated with bin Laden's group, links jihadists across much of North Africa. Somalia has been a failed state for more than two decades. Islamist extremists now control much of the south and center of the country. The rise in piracy off the Somalia cost is both a symptom and a source of jihadist activity. The collapse of the Somali economy, particularly its fishing industry, has encouraged young men to become pirates. The proceeds of their activities fund Islamic groups operating in the country. The risk of extremist activity spilling over the border into neighboring Kenya remains considerable.

Even more troubling than the extent of al-Qaeda's network is the strength of its ideology. Osama bin Laden remains popular on the streets of many Muslim countries, especially in the Arab world. After 9/11 journalist-turned novelist Rick Mofina saw a young boy in Nigeria wearing a t-shirt with a picture of Osama bin Laden and words proclaiming him number 1 hero.[27] The U.S. has had little success countering his ideology among the young, poor, and disenfranchised. American actions during seven years of the Global War on Terrorism have probably made matters worse, deepening anger at U.S. unilateralism and heavy handedness. Things may, however, be changing. On June 4, 2009, President Obama delivered an historic address to the Muslim world at one of its oldest seats of learning, the Cairo University. He acknowledged the deep tension and mistrust that exists between the U.S. and Muslims. Without backing away from America's commitment to fight terrorism or its historic ties to Israel, he appealed to his audience for better relations. "I've come here to

Cairo to seek a new beginning between the United States and Muslims around the world," he declared, "one based on mutual interest and mutual respect, and one based upon the truth that America and Islam are not exclusive and need not be in competition.[28] The speech was well received by those in attendance but received mixed reviews from those who heard via the media. Commentators in the Muslim world viewed it with cautious optimism, waiting to see when and if words would become deeds.

Among those paying closest attention to the President's speech was Osama bin Laden, who tried to pre-empt it with a statement of his own issued the day before Obama spoke in Cairo. In a taped message sent to Al Jazeera, bin Laden declared that President Obama had "sowed new seeds of hatred against America."[29] He reminded his audience that as the President prepared to speak Pakistani forces acting on America's behalf was displacing thousands of Muslims from their homes in the Swat Valley. Less important than his words was Osama's timing. He recognized in the new President's extended hand of friendship a threat to al-Qaeda potentially more dangerous than all of George W. Bush's military actions.

NOTES

1. Osama bin Laden, in Peter Bergen, The *Osama bin Laden I Know* (New York: Free Press, 2006), p. 283.
2. Sulayman Abu Ghaith, quoted in ibid., p. 284.
3. Interview with Osama Bin Ladin by unidentified Ummat special correspondent, in *Compilation of Usama Bin Ladin Statements 1994 - January 2004* (Washington, DC: 2004), p. 178.
4. Excerpts of al-Qaeda tape aired on al-Jazeera, aired April 18, 2002, in ibid., pp. 192-193.
5. Ibid., p. 193.
6. Hamid Mir, in Bergen, *The Osama bin Laden I Know*, p. 287.
7. Sayf Adel, quoted in Sarah E. Zaibel, *The Military Strategy of Global Jihad* (Carlisle Barracks, PA: US Army War College Strategic Studies Institute, 2007). p. 6. http://www.StrategicStudiesInstitute.army.mil/, accessed July 22, 2009.
8. Vahid Mojdeh, in Bergen, *The Osama bin Laden I Know.*, p. 325.
9. Peter Jouvenal, in ibid., p. 323.
10. Osama bin Laden statement aired, October 7, 2001, in Raymond Ibrahim, *The Al Qaeda Reader* (New York: Broadway Books, 2007), p. 194.

11. See Sean Naylor, *Not a Good Day to Die: The Untold Story of Operation Anaconda* (New York: Penguin, 2006).
12. Peter Jouvenal, in Bergen, *The Osama bin Laden I Know*, p. 331.
13. Mohammed Musa, in ibid., p. 330.
14. Riedel, *Search for Al-Qaeda*, pp. 121-122.
15. Osama bin Laden, in Bergen, *The Osama bin Laden I Know*, p. 337.
16. Osama bin Laden, Transcript of statement on al Jazeera television, November 12, 2002, in *Compilation of Usama Bin Ladin Statements*, p. 227.
17. Transcript of al Jazeera broadcast, in ibid., p. 270.
18. Details of Madrid bombing from MIPT Terrorism Data Base, available at http://www.terrorisminfo.mipt.org/incidentcalendar.asp, accessed June 17, 2009.
19. Osama bin Laden, "Osama bin Laden's Peace Treaty Offer to the Europeans," in Raymond Ibrahim, *The Al Qaeda Reader* (New York: Broadway Books, 2007), p. 234.
20. *Report of the Official Account of the Bombings in London on 7th July 2005* (London: Her Majesty's Stationary Office, 2006), p. 20.
21. Ayman al-Zawahiri, in Ibrahim Raymond, *The Al Qaeda Reader* (New York: Broadway Books, 2007), p. 238.
22. Lawrence Wright, *The Looming Tower: Al-Qaeda and the Road to 9/11* (New York: Knopf, 2006), p. 318.
23. Osama bin Laden, message televised on Al Jazeera, October 18, 2003, in *Compilation of Usama Bin Ladin Statements*, p. 211.
24. Osama bin Laden, message televised on Al Jazeera, October 2004, in ibid., p. 217.
25. Osama bin Laden, taped message, January 2006, in ibid., p. 221.
26. "Bundestagwahl im Visier von al-Qaieda," *Die Welt*, Sunday, July 5, 2009, p.4.
27. Rick Mofina, *Six Seconds* (New York: Mira Books, 2009), p. 471.
28. President Barack Obama, Transcript of Cairo University Speech, available at http://www.whitehouse.gov/the_press_office/Remarks-by-the-President-at-Cairo-University-6-04-09/, accessed June 20, 2009.
29. Osama bin Laden, quoted in, "Bin Laden Attacks Obama Policies," Al Jazeera English net, http://english.aljazeera.net/news/middleeast/2009/06/200963123251920623.html, accessed June 20, 2009.

CONCLUSION

BIN LADEN'S DEATH

A half hour after midnight on Monday, May 2, 2011, two helicopters deployed twenty-five members of S.E.A.L. (SEA-Air-Land) Team 6, the Navy's elite counter-terrorism force, to a compound in Abbattobad, Pakistan. The team stormed its main building and in a second-story bedroom they shot and killed the world's most wanted man. Osama bin Laden was fifty-four years old. He had spent much of the previous decade in hiding, perhaps living as much as five years of it in the comfortable compound with members of his family under the nose of the Pakistani Army, whose military academy stands nearby. Although the White House decided against releasing photos of the dead terrorist leader for fear of inflaming the passions of his supporters, no serious observer questioned his death. A few days after the raid, al-Qaeda confirmed that its founder was gone.

The killing of bin Laden was a triumph of intelligence gathering, a brilliant operation, a public relations coup, and a satisfying act of justice. Very few people died in the raid (two men and a woman were also killed) and only two people were wounded.[1] No American suffered so much as a scratch. The SEALs spirited away his body and buried it at sea within the 24 hours proscribed by Islamic law, denying him a hero's funeral and a martyr's shrine. Crowds gathered at ground zero in New York City to celebrate the news. The raid also produced an intelligence bonanza garnered from captured computer hard drives, DVDs and written notes. The information they contain should help the U.S. and its allies foil terrorist plots and capture or kill more al-Qaeda members.

The raid on bin Laden's compound allowed analysts to fill in some of the details of his life after 9/11. He had been in deep hiding since his escape from Tora Bora, Afghanistan in December 2001. Neither his outlook nor his objectives changed during those years. His statements smuggled out from hiding places contained no new ideas and shed no new light on his thinking because there was no new light to shed. Osama's journey to the dark side was completed sometime between 1992 and 1996 when the last elements of his worldview fell into place. As a youth he had chosen the path of a devout, Muslim. His high school gym teacher exposed him to the ideas of radical Islam. This exposure deepened his piety and made him more conservative, but they did not change how he lived. In classic fashion he pursued the greater jihad of leading a righteous life. By all accounts he was a good husband to his four wives and a loving father to all of his children. His religious beliefs, however, had no political dimension. They began to acquire that dimension when he attended King Abdul Aziz University. Although he studied economics, he never earned a degree. He did, however, attend lectures by Mohammed Qutb and read the classic works of Mohammed's martyred brother Sayid.

The ideas of the Egyptian Muslim Brotherhood that the Qutb brothers taught attracted bin Laden to the radical Islamist cause, but they did not launch him on the course of jihad. The Afghan War against the Soviets provided a cause upon which to focus his religious zeal, but he would probably not have embraced it without the encouragement of Abdulla Azzam. Even then his major contribution to the jihad was not as a fighter but as a funder and facilitator helping other foreign mujahedeen journey to Afghanistan.

The step from recruiter to holy warrior was easily taken and perhaps inevitable. Bin Laden had always been a doer. Never satisfied to watch or merely direct, Osama needed to act. He lacked the experience and training to be accepted as a commander by the seasoned Afghan fighters, so he raised his own force of Arab mujahedeen and led them into battle. They performed poorly and they made a negligible contribution to the war.

They did, however, provide the core of a future terrorist group, and they helped to create the bin Laden myth. The Afghan Arabs became recruits for al-Qaeda, and Osama returned home to find himself lionized by Saudis who wished to hear of his exploits.

Despite its enormous role in shaping his worldview, the Afghan war did not guarantee that bin would become a terrorist. Had circumstances been different, he might have returned to the quiet life of a Saudi businessman following a brief time as a minor celebrity. The Gulf War eliminated that prospect. Osama never got over his bitter disappointment at the Saudi monarchy's refusal to accept his offer of a mujahedeen army to defend the kingdom and expel Saddam Hussein from Kuwait. When he went into voluntary exile in Sudan, he entered a hornet's nest of radical Islamist jihadism that completed his extremist education. By the time he left Khartoum in 1996, he was committed to global jihad against apostate Muslim regimes, the U.S., which supported those governments, and America's allies around the world

AL-QAEDA AFTER BIN LADEN

Bin Laden's death should have far less impact on al-Qaeda than it would have had he been removed in 1998 or even 2001. The terrorist group is not as hierarchically organized as it once was. Experts now refer to "al-Qaeda central" to distinguish the organization in Pakistan from its worldwide network of cells and affiliates. While al-Qaeda central has recovered from the disruption of the 2002 invasion of Afghanistan, its need to operate underground has probably forced it to become more decentralized even in its Pakistani safe haven than it did when it functioned openly in Kandahar. Al-Qaeda has long had a deep pool of leadership talent and a seemingly inexhaustible supply of new recruits. The loss of one leader may provide a temporary disruption but will probably not be fatal in the long run. Anyone who believes otherwise would do well to remember L. Paul Bremer's gleeful announcement on the capture of Saddam Husain ("We got him!") and how little his capture effected the insurgency.

Bin Laden's precise role in the organization remains unclear. Virtually all experts acknowledge his importance as a fundraiser and spokesman.

This prominence and the American efforts to demonize him in the aftermath of the East Africa Embassy bombings increased his public relations value enormously. Much of the Arab street still considers him a hero, and at least some of his associates have described him as "charismatic," although this conclusion is by no means a consensus. What remains less clear is the role Osama has played in the day-to-day operation of al-Qaeda. His more public role in the Afghan war against the Soviets does not speak well of his organizational ability. He was not the brains behind the Service Office. His one seemingly independent venture, the creation of an Afghan Arab contingent capable of fighting independently, was poorly conceived and badly executed. It may well be that the other foreign mujahedeen tolerated him for the money he brought them. He was a founding member of al-Qaeda but does not seem to have designed its structure or entirely directed its activities. It is debatable whether he or al-Zawahiri took it global. He may have lent it some of his indefatigable energy and was invaluable during the 1990s as its public face. However, those contributions no longer matter as much now that the global jihad has been launched. In sum, while al-Qaeda did not wish to lose Osama bin Laden, they can certainly do without him.

Intelligence gathered in the raid that killed him reveals that bin Laden may have been more involved in operational activities than previously thought, reviewing plans and possibly approving them. However, the need to avoid using electronic communications, which might be traced, hampered his ability to communicate with the rest of al-Qaeda's leadership. He probably did not run the organization on a day-to-day basis. In the final analysis, Osama bin Laden may have been more useful to the movement as a myth than as a man. Release of videos captured during the S.E.A.L. raid, however, may tarnish his carefully polished image. One shows a frail, narcissistic bin Laden huddled in a blanket watching himself on TV, and another reveals him stumbling through a speech he is practicing.

PORTRAIT OF A TERRORIST

What has hopefully emerged from this account is the outline of a person, a portrait of his organization, an analysis of his heroic myth, and an understanding of the larger ideological movement to which he belongs. A biography of Osama bin Laden detailing even the majority of his life may never be possible. Future historians will have more sources than contemporary ones, but it seems doubtful that these documents will shed much light on his formative early years. The recollections of those who knew him are what writers have today and probably all that they will have in the future. His family members have maintained a conspiracy of silence about their wayward member, who is undoubtedly bad for business. It remains to be seen whether any of them will be more forthcoming in the years ahead. Perhaps years from now one of this children or grandchildren will fill in the huge gaps in his life that Western writers currently encounter.

Even with the limitations of available evidence, however, it is possible to identify formative events that shaped bin Laden's character and personality. The death of Mohammed bin Laden when Osama was only nine seems to have profoundly impacted the child's psyche. Mohammed had been a stern but loving father whom his young son revered. His death created a void that would be hard to fill. Bin Laden's later impressionability and need for approval may stem from this early loss. His high school gym teacher, Mohammed Qutb, Abdullah Azzam, and Ayman al-Zawahiri each in turn exploited this impressionability. On the other hand, Mohammed spent relatively little time with Osama, and many children lose fathers at an early age without growing up to become terrorists. In the patriarch's extended family young Osama should have had plenty of positive male role models and good mentors to take the place of his father. Since the al-Qaeda leader never underwent psychotherapy, developing a completely accurate psychological profile of him will never be possible.

Nevertheless, this study does make possible some tentative conclusions about the personality of history's most infamous terrorist. By all accounts, Osama bin Laden was a shy, unassuming young man. His teachers credit him with above average intelligence, but he only earned average grades. His unwillingness to speak up in class no doubt hurt his academic performance. He appears to have been well mannered and honest. He showed no violent tendencies growing up, nor was he even particularly competitive. Members of his soccer team describe him as a talented but indifferent player. Beyond these superficial observations, the only thing acquaintances seem to remember about Osama was his unusual height.

A somewhat larger body of sources documents the evolution of bin Laden's religious worldview. He was clearly more devout than most of his siblings and friends, although none of them found his piety unusual or problematic. It seems that every wealthy Saudi family produced at least one Osama. Bin Laden's worldview blended Saudi Wahabism with the radical Islamism of the Muslim Brotherhood articulated most fully by Sayid Qutb. Qutb convinced bin Laden of the need for a purely Islamic answer to the problem of modernity, a way to reconcile modern technology with traditional Muslim belief and practice.

Qutb did not, however, provide bin Laden the ideological impetus for jihad. Like most members of the Muslim Brotherhood, he preferred to work within legitimate politics, gaining power through the ballot box not the gun or the bomb. His successor Ayman al-Zawahiri did not share this evolutionary view. The execution of Qutb, brutal suppression of the Brotherhood, and his own torture at the hands of the Egyptian security services following the assassination of President Anwar Sadat convinced him that Islamism could never triumph through the democratic process. His al-Jihad organization broke with the Brotherhood on the issue of violence. Zawahiri also believed, contrary to traditional Islamic teaching, that the *Quran* permitted violent overthrow of apostate regimes. Zawahiri completed bin Laden's jihadist education, beginning in Pakistan during the Afghan war against the Soviets and concluding in Sudan during Osama's voluntary exile there.

THE TIMES AND THE MAN

I began this study with a question that perennially vexes historians: do individuals make history or do circumstances call forth individuals? In the case of Osama bin Laden the second answer seems more accurate. Events shaped him more than he shaped them, and had he not stepped up to become the face of al-Qaeda, someone else almost certainly would have. He may have had some ability to get diverse groups and individuals to work together, but he was probably not responsible for organizing the group and showed little interest in its day to day functions. Al-Qaeda's most successful attacks were conceived and planned by others, although he probably had to approve them. Bin Laden was also not an original thinker. His pronouncements, which he may not have written himself, contain a generic list of Islamist grievances and platitudes. The evolution of his thought can be traced by recounting the list of radicals with whom he came in contact. Even his alleged charisma is suspect. Prior to his emergence on the world stage, no one seems to have described bin Laden as charismatic. After he achieved notoriety, few people got close enough to him to find out. Those who did were either already committed to jihad or journalists invited in for carefully staged and closely scripted interviews.

In her thought provoking study, *A Hundred Osamas*, Sherifa Zuhur makes a compelling case that the Islamist talent pool is so deep that the movement will have no trouble replacing any number of leaders killed or captured by the U.S. She cites the case of Abu Musab al-Zarqawi as an example. In September 2003, Zarqawi created the Organization for Jihad in the Land of the two rivers, generally dubbed "Al-Qaeda in Iraq." This organization wreaked havoc in Iraq for three years before the U.S. killed Zarqawi by bombing his safe house. The main al-Qaeda organization regrouping in Pakistan did not create Zarqawi's group. He chose to link up with them. For a few years, he even eclipsed Osama bin Laden in the media. Once again, the event (U.S. invasion of Iraq) called forth the man. Perhaps only timing and circumstances kept Zarqawi from the lead role bin Laden got to play.[2]

Had Osama bin Laden been born in economically disadvantaged circumstances and yet developed the same convictions, he would probably still have been recruited to the jihadist cause but perhaps in a very different capacity. In many respects he fit the profile of the ideal suicide bomber. He was a deeply impressionable young man, unswervingly loyal to his convictions and to those who shared them. Possessed of an unshakable faith and unflinching courage, he genuinely believed that he acted on God's behalf and would be rewarded for his service to the cause, convictions he shared with everyone who ever blew himself up in the name of God.

In the final analysis bin Laden's most important contribution to al-Qaeda, besides the considerable resources he commanded, may be his role as mythic hero. From streets to palaces he has become the symbol and embodiment of opposition for all those Muslims who see Islam under siege or whose aspirations for a better life are blocked by circumstances beyond their control. His willingness to forgo a life of ease in Saudi Arabia earned him the respect of many whose suffering and want are hardly matters of choice. Countering the threat posed by such a leader lies not in killing him but in removing the circumstances that called him forth and made him a hero.

NOTES

1. Casualty figures and details of raid from, "US Releases bin Laden Videos," BBC online, May 6, 2011, available at http://www.bbc.co.uk/news/world-south-asia-13257330, accessed May 7, 2011.
2. Sherifa Zuhur, *A Hundred Osamas: Islamist Threats and the Future of Counterinsurgency* (Carlisle Barracks, PA: Strategic Studies Institute, U.S. Army War College, 2005).

APPENDIX

SELECTED DOCUMENTS

The documents in this section represent a small percentage of the sources used to produce this book. To facilitate understanding, a brief commentary precedes each source. The sources are arranged chronologically, illustrating how the United States understanding of al-Qaeda and the threat it poses has evolved over time.

DOCUMENT 1

The 1997 *Patterns of Global Terrorism Report* makes scant mention of Osama bin Laden but does acknowledge his influence on and contribution to terrorist activities around the world. The report does not seem to consider him a serious threat to the U.S. The report is available at http://www.hri.org/docs/USSD-Terror/97/asia.html

AFGHANISTAN

Islamic extremists from around the world—including large numbers of Egyptians, Algerians, Palestinians, and Saudis—continued to use Afghanistan as a training ground and home base from which to operate in 1997. The Taliban, as well as many of the other combatants in the

Afghan civil war, facilitated the operation of training and indoctrination facilities for non-Afghans in the territories they controlled. Several Afghani factions also provided logistic support, free passage, and sometimes passports to the members of various terrorist organizations. These individuals, in turn, were involved in fighting in Bosnia and Herzegovina, Chechnya, Tajikistan, Kashmir, the Philippines, and parts of the Middle East.

Saudi-born terrorist financier Usama Bin Ladin relocated from Jalalabad to the Taliban's capital of Qandahar in early 1997 and established a new base of operations. He continued to incite violence against the United States, particularly against US forces in Saudi Arabia. Bin Ladin called on Muslims to retaliate against the US prosecutor in the Mir Aimal Kansi trial for disparaging comments he made about Pakistanis and praised the Pakistan-based Kashmiri group HUA in the wake of its formal designation as a foreign terrorist organization by the United States. According to the Pakistani press, following Kansi's rendition to the United States, Bin Ladin warned the United States that, if it attempted his capture, he would "teach them a lesson similar to the lesson they were taught in Somalia."

DOCUMENT 2

The East Africa embassy bombings brought Osama bin Laden to the attention of the American public. Although al-Qaeda had been in existence for almost a decade, bin Laden was added to the American terrorism list only after the August 1998 attacks in Nairobi and Darussalam. The text of the report is available at http://www.state.gov/www/global/terrorism/1998Report/intro.html#foot1

Following the bombings of the two US Embassies in East Africa, the US Government obtained evidence implicating Usama Bin Ladin's network in the attacks. To preempt additional attacks, the United States launched military strikes against terrorist targets in Afghanistan and Sudan on 20 August. That same day, President Clinton amended Executive Order 12947 to add Usama Bin Ladin and his key associates to the list of terrorists, thus blocking their US assets-including property and bank accounts-and prohibiting all US financial transactions with them. As a result of what Attorney General Janet Reno called the most extensive overseas criminal investigation in US history, and working closely with the Kenyan and Tanzanian Governments, the US Government indicted Bin Ladin and 11 of his associates for the two bombings and other terrorist crimes. Several suspects were brought to the United States to stand trial. The Department of State announced a reward of up to $5 million for information leading to the arrest or conviction of any of the suspects anywhere in the world.

DOCUMENT 3

Osama bin Laden's 1998 fatwa is a declaration of war against the U.S. and its allies. It represents the culmination of his political/religious worldview. The document is available at http://www.fas.org/irp/world/para/docs/980223-fatwa.htm

Jihad Against Jews and Crusaders
World Islamic Front Statement
23 February 1998
Shaykh Usamah Bin-Muhammad Bin-Ladin
Ayman al-Zawahiri, amir of the Jihad Group in Egypt
Abu-Yasir Rifa'i Ahmad Taha, Egyptian Islamic Group
Shaykh Mir Hamzah, secretary of the Jamiat-ul-Ulema-e-Pakistan
Fazlur Rahman, amir of the Jihad Movement in Bangladesh

Praise be to Allah, who revealed the Book, controls the clouds, defeats factionalism, and says in His Book: "But when the forbidden months are past, then fight and slay the pagans wherever ye find them, seize them, beleaguer them, and lie in wait for them in every stratagem (of war)"; and peace be upon our Prophet, Muhammad Bin-'Abdallah, who said: I have been sent with the sword between my hands to ensure that no one but Allah is worshipped, Allah who put my livelihood under the shadow of my spear and who inflicts humiliation and scorn on those who disobey my orders.

The Arabian Peninsula has never—since Allah made it flat, created its desert, and encircled it with seas—been stormed by any forces like the crusader armies spreading in it like locusts, eating its riches and wiping out its plantations. All this is happening at a time in which nations are attacking Muslims like people fighting over a plate of food. In the light of the grave situation and the lack of support, we and you are obliged to discuss current events, and we should all agree on how to settle the matter.

No one argues today about three facts that are known to everyone; we will list them, in order to remind everyone:

First, for over seven years the United States has been occupying the lands of Islam in the holiest of places, the Arabian Peninsula, plundering its riches, dictating to its rulers, humiliating its people, terrorizing its neighbors, and turning its bases in the Peninsula into a spearhead through which to fight the neighboring Muslim peoples.

If some people have in the past argued about the fact of the occupation, all the people of the Peninsula have now acknowledged it. The best proof of this is the Americans' continuing aggression against the Iraqi people using the Peninsula as a staging post, even though all its rulers are against their territories being used to that end, but they are helpless.

Second, despite the great devastation inflicted on the Iraqi people by the crusader-Zionist alliance, and despite the huge number of those killed, which has exceeded 1 million... despite all this, the Americans are once against trying to repeat the horrific massacres, as though they are not content with the protracted blockade imposed after the ferocious war or the fragmentation and devastation.

So here they come to annihilate what is left of this people and to humiliate their Muslim neighbors.

Third, if the Americans' aims behind these wars are religious and economic, the aim is also to serve the Jews' petty state and divert attention from its occupation of Jerusalem and murder of Muslims there. The best proof of this is their eagerness to destroy Iraq, the strongest neighboring Arab state, and their endeavor to fragment all the states of the region such as Iraq, Saudi Arabia, Egypt, and Sudan into paper statelets and through their disunion and weakness to guarantee Israel's survival and the continuation of the brutal crusade occupation of the Peninsula. All these crimes and sins committed by the Americans are a clear declaration of war on Allah, his messenger, and Muslims. And ulema have throughout Islamic history unanimously agreed that the jihad is an individual duty if the enemy destroys the Muslim countries. This was revealed by Imam

Bin-Qadamah in "Al- Mughni," Imam al-Kisa'i in "Al-Bada'i," al-Qurtubi in his interpretation, and the shaykh of al-Islam in his books, where he said: "As for the fighting to repulse [an enemy], it is aimed at defending sanctity and religion, and it is a duty as agreed [by the ulema]. Nothing is more sacred than belief except repulsing an enemy who is attacking religion and life."

On that basis, and in compliance with Allah's order, we issue the following fatwa to all Muslims: The ruling to kill the Americans and their allies—civilians and military—is an individual duty for every Muslim who can do it in any country in which it is possible to do it, in order to liberate the al-Aqsa Mosque and the holy mosque [Mecca] from their grip, and in order for their armies to move out of all the lands of Islam, defeated and unable to threaten any Muslim. This is in accordance with the words of Almighty Allah, "and fight the pagans all together as they fight you all together," and "fight them until there is no more tumult or oppression, and there prevail justice and faith in Allah."

This is in addition to the words of Almighty Allah: "And why should ye not fight in the cause of Allah and of those who, being weak, are ill-treated (and oppressed)?—women and children, whose cry is: 'Our Lord, rescue us from this town, whose people are oppressors; and raise for us from thee one who will help!' "

We—with Allah's help—call on every Muslim who believes in Allah and wishes to be rewarded to comply with Allah's order to kill the Americans and plunder their money wherever and whenever they find it. We also call on Muslim ulema, leaders, youths, and soldiers to launch the raid on Satan's U.S. troops and the devil's supporters allying with them, and to displace those who are behind them so that they may learn a lesson.

Almighty Allah said: "O ye who believe, give your response to Allah and His Apostle, when He calleth you to that which will give you life. And know that Allah cometh between a man and his heart, and that it is He to whom ye shall all be gathered."

Almighty Allah also says: "O ye who believe, what is the matter with you, that when ye are asked to go forth in the cause of Allah, ye cling so heavily to the earth! Do ye prefer the life of this world to the hereafter? But little is the comfort of this life, as compared with the hereafter. Unless ye go forth, He will punish you with a grievous penalty, and put others in your place; but Him ye would not harm in the least. For Allah hath power over all things."

Almighty Allah also says: "So lose no heart, nor fall into despair. For ye must gain mastery if ye are true in faith."

DOCUMENT 4

A Grand Jury indicted bin Laden and his associates for the East Africa bombing. Following is the introduction to the indictment and its first count. The entire document is available at http://fl1.findlaw.com/news.findlaw.com/hdocs/docs/binladen/usbinladen1.pdf

The Grand Jury charges:

Background: al-Qaeda

1. At all relevant times from in or about 1989 until the date of the filing of this Indictment, an international terrorist group existed which was dedicated to opposing non-Islamic governments with force and violence. This organization grew out of the "mekhtab al khidemat" (the "Services Office") organization which had maintained offices in various parts of the world, including Afghanistan, Pakistan (particularly in Peshawar) and the United States, particularly at the Alkifah Refugee Center in Brooklyn, New York. The group was founded by defendants USAMA BIN LADEN and MUHAMMAD ATEF, a/k/a "Abu Hafs al Masry," together with "Abu Ubaidah al Banshiri" and others. From in or about 1989 until the present, the group called itself "al Qaeda" ("the Base"). From 1989 until in or about 1991, the group (hereafter referred to as "al Qaeda") was headquartered in Afghanistan and Peshawar, Pakistan. In or about 1991, the leadership of al Qaeda, including its "emir" (or prince) defendant USAMA BIN LADEN, relocated to the Sudan. Al Qaeda was headquartered in the Sudan from approximately 1991 until approximately 1996 but still maintained offices in various parts of the world. In 1996, defendants USAMA BIN LADEN and MUHAMMAD ATEF and other members of al Qaeda relocated to Afghanistan. At all relevant times, al Qaeda was led by its emir, defendant USAMA BIN LADEN. Members of al Qaeda pledged an

oath of allegiance (called a "bayat") to defendant USAMA BIN LADEN and al Qaeda. Those who were suspected of collaborating against al Qaeda were to be identified and killed.

2. Al Qaeda opposed the United States for several reasons. First, the United States was regarded as an "infidel" because it was not governed in a manner consistent with the group's extremist interpretation of Islam. Second, the United States was viewed as providing essential support for other "infidel" governments and institutions, particularly the governments of Saudi Arabia and Egypt, the nation of Israel and the United Nations organization, which were regarded as enemies of the group. Third, al Qaeda opposed the involvement of the United States armed forces in the Gulf War in 1991 and in Operation Restore Hope in Somalia in 1992 and 1993, which were viewed by al Qaeda as pretextual preparations for an American occupation of Islamic countries. In particular, al Qaeda opposed the continued presence of American military forces in Saudi Arabia (and elsewhere on the Saudi Arabian peninsula) following the Gulf War. Fourth, al Qaeda opposed the United States Government because of the arrest, conviction and imprisonment of persons belonging to al Qaeda or its affiliated terrorist groups or with whom it worked, including Sheik Omar Abdel Rahman.
3. One of the principal goals of al Qaeda was to drive the United States armed forces out of Saudi Arabia (and elsewhere on the Saudi Arabian peninsula) and Somalia by violence. Members of al Qaeda issued fatwahs (rulings on Islamic law) indicating that such attacks were both proper and necessary.
4. From in or about 1993, until in or about December 1999, AYMAN AL ZAWAHIRI, a/k/a "Abdel Muaz," a/k/a "Dr. Ayman al Zawahiri," a/k/a "the Doctor," a/k/a "Nur," a/k/a "Ustaz," a/k/a "Abu Mohammed," a/k/a "Abu Mohammed Nur al-Deen," led the Egyptian Islamic Jihad which was dedicated to the forceful overthrow of the Egyptian Government and to violent opposition of the United States, in part, for its support of the Government in Egypt. Members of Egyptian Islamic Jihad also pledged allegiance to AL ZAWAHIRI and Egyptian Islamic Jihad. Many of the leading members of the Egyptian Islamic Jihad became influential members of al Qaeda, including

defendants AYMAN AL ZAWAHIRI and MUHAMMAD ATEF. Eventually, by at least in or about February 1998, the Egyptian Islamic Jihad led by AL ZAWAHIRI had effectively merged with al Qaeda and the Egyptian Islamic Jihad joined with al Qaeda in targeting American civilians.

5. Al Qaeda functioned both on its own and through some of the terrorist organizations that operated under its umbrella, including: Egyptian Islamic Jihad, and at times, the Islamic Group (also known as "el Gamaa Islamia" or simply "Gamaa't"), led by Sheik Omar Abdel Rahman and later by Ahmed Refai Taha, a/k/a "Abu Yasser al Masri," named as co-conspirators but not as defendants herein; and a number of jihad groups in other countries, including the Sudan, Egypt, Saudi Arabia, Yemen, Somalia, Eritrea, Djibouti, Afghanistan, Pakistan, Bosnia, Croatia, Albania, Algeria, Tunisia, Lebanon, the Philippines, Tajikistan, Azerbaijan and the Kashmiri region of India and the Chechnyan region of Russia. Al Qaeda also maintained cells and personnel in a number of countries to facilitate its activities, including in Kenya, Tanzania, the United Kingdom, Canada and the United States.
6. Al Qaeda had a command and control structure which included a majlis al shura (or consultation council) which discussed and approved major undertakings, including terrorist operations. The defendants USAMA BIN LADEN, MUHAMMAD ATEF, a/k/a "Abu Hafs," AYMAN AL ZAWAHIRI, SAIF AL ADEL, MAMDOUH MAHMUD SALIM, a/k/a "Abu Hajer," and ABDULLAH AHMED ABDULLAH, a/k/a "Abu Mohamed el Masry," a/k/a "Saleh," among others, sat on the majlis al shura (or consultation council) of al Qaeda. Egyptian Islamic Jihad had a Founding Council, on which the defendant IBRAHIM EIDAROUS sat.
7. Al Qaeda also had a "military committee" which considered and approved "military" matters. MUHAMMAD ATEF, a/k/a "Abu Hafs," the defendant, sat on the military committee and was one of defendant USAMA BIN LADEN's two principal military commanders together with "Abu Ubaidah al Banshiri," until the death of "Abu Ubaidah al Banshiri" in May 1996. Among his other duties, MUHAMMAD ATEF, a/k/a "Abu Hafs," the defendant, had the principal responsibility for supervising the training of al Qaeda

members. SAIF AL ADEL also served on the military committee, reporting to MUHAMMAD ATEF, a/k/a "Abu Hafs."

8. USAMA BIN LADEN, the defendant, and al Qaeda also forged alliances with the National Islamic Front in the Sudan and with representatives of the government of Iran, and its associated terrorist group Hizballah, for the purpose of working together against their perceived common enemies in the West, particularly the United States.
9. In or about 1994, the defendant USAMA BIN LADEN, working together with KHALID AL FAWWAZ, a/k/a "Khaled Abdul Rahman Hamad al Fawwaz," a/k/a "Abu Omar," a/k/a "Hamad," set up a media information office in London, England (hereafter the "London office"), which was designed both to publicize the statements of USAMA BIN LADEN and to provide a cover for activity in support of al Qaeda's "military" activities, including the recruitment of military trainees, the disbursement of funds and the procurement of necessary equipment (including satellite telephones) and necessary services. In addition, the London office served as a conduit for messages, including reports on military and security matters from various al Qaeda cells, including the Kenyan cell, to al Qaeda's headquarters.

COUNTS ONE THROUGH SIX:
CONSPIRACIES TO MURDER, BOMB AND MAIM
COUNT ONE:
CONSPIRACY TO KILL UNITED STATES NATIONALS

10. From at least 1991 until the date of the filing of this Indictment, in the Southern District of New York, in Afghanistan, the United Kingdom, Pakistan, the Sudan, Saudi Arabia, Yemen, Somalia, Kenya, Tanzania, Azerbaijan, the Philippines and elsewhere out of the jurisdiction of any particular state or district, USAMA BIN LADEN, . . . [list of other defendants], defendants, at least one of whom was first brought to and arrested in the Southern District of New York, together with other members and associates of al Qaeda, Egyptian Islamic Jihad and others known and unknown to the Grand Jury, unlawfully, wilfully and knowingly combined, conspired, confederated and agreed to kill nationals of the United States.

DOCUMENT 5

On October 3, 2001, the Committee on International Relations of the U.S. House of Representatives met to consider the threat posed by al-Qaeda. Following is a prepared statement presented to the committee. The statements provide an indication what the U.S. intelligence committee knew at the time of the 9/11 attacks. Their picture of bin Laden and his organization was incomplete and inaccurate. This statement and the transcript of the entire meeting may be found at http://www.internationalrelations.house.gov/archives/107/75562.pdf

PREPARED STATEMENT OF VINCENT CANNISTRARO, FORMER CHIEF OF COUNTERTERRORISM OPERATIONS, CENTRAL INTELLIGENCE AGENCY

I am pleased to appear before this committee to provide my views on al-Qaeda, its structure and its objectives. It is important to note that Americans have a difficult time in understanding extremist organizations with a religious orientation like al-Qaeda. It is essential that the agencies of our government involved in law enforcement and intelligence become intimately familiar with the culture of religious zealots whether of foreign or domestic origin. We must understand the nature of the threat before we can successfully confront it. In America, we also have fundamentalists such as Christian Identity, and other religious extremists who kill or maim in the name of God. Comprehending the danger and the mind-set of these groups is a first step to deterring the violence executed by the Osama Bin Laden's of the world. Unless we know what drives these religious extremists, who are willing to kill themselves in the performance of their violent acts, we will see days like September 11, 2001, repeated, perhaps with even greater casualties. It is worth studying the evolution of the al-Qaeda group. Bin Laden, who opposes the American influence in the Middle East, was outraged by the 1990 Persian Gulf War which saw American and other western troops stationed in Saudi Arabia. Bin Laden considers the country, ruled by the Al-Sau'd family, as the guardian of the Islamic holy places. King Abd'al aziz al-Sau'd, who founded the monarchy, had the support of the Wahabis, the fundamentalist Islamic sect. The al-Sau'd monarchy derives its authority from the Wahabis, who allied with Abd'al aziz, in creating modern Saudi Arabia. In return, the monarchy serves to guarantee the sanctity of Mecca and Medina, the site and magnetic pole for pilgrimages by the world's Muslims. In Bin Laden's view, the Saudi monarchy betrayed that sacred pact by allowing Christian and Jewish soldiers to be stationed on the soil of this Islamic country which had been entrusted with a special protectorate mission for the holy places. Bin Laden's opposition to the monarch resulted in his expulsion from the Kingdom. Shortly after, Bin Laden used his personal fortune and continuing contributions from wealthy Islamic businessmen in Saudi and the Gulf to organize training camps in the Sudan for Islamic activists from every major Islamic country. These contributions, plus revenues from Islamic Charity fronts, such as the International Islamic Relief Organization, headed by Bin Laden's brother-in-law, as well as numerous other charitable fronts, continue to fuel his group today

The international cadres that comprise many of the networks associated with al-Qaeda, were trained by so-called "Arab-Afghans" with fighting experience from the Soviet-Afghan war, although many of these "mujahedin" did not reach Afghanistan until after the Soviet withdrawal in 1989. The main mission for Bin Laden was to disperse trained fighters to their native lands to fight against the secular Arab regimes and replace them with religious governments based on the Sharia-Islamic rather than civil law. The targets were secular Muslim countries such as Egypt and Algeria, and Muslim dominated provinces such as Chechnya and Dagestan in Russia and in Bosnia and Kosovo. Anti-government movements were also promoted in Libya and Tunisia as well. Indeed, Bin Laden's vision is to re-establish the "Islamic Caliphate" across every Muslim country, a religious restoration of the old Ottoman Empire, this time under the leadership of the Taliban leader, Mullah Omar. Usama sees the United States and its world influence as the principal obstacle to achieving his vision.

Bin Laden relocated his operations to Afghanistan following pressure on the Sudan exerted by Saudi Arabia and the U.S. The Taliban, a group of religious students from Pakistani schools, were successful in establishing control over Afghanistan with the active military support of Pakistan's military intelligence service, the Inter Services Directorate (ISI). Pakistan's concern was to promote ethnic Pashtun control over the country, which was being run by Afghans hostile to Pashtun rule and Pakistani influence. The Pashtuns, or Pathans in common western usage, designates several dozen separate tribes on both sides of the Afghan/Pakistani border. The Taliban, lacking a secular education, is almost medieval in its concept of governance. The Taliban rulers have mismanaged the country, but have been amenable to Pakistani political influence although not totally subservient to it. Pakistan has also used its position and support to the Taliban to establish within Afghanistan a series of training camps for Kashmiri terrorists. ISI personnel are present, in mufti, to conduct the training. This arrangement allowed Pakistan "plausible denial" that it is promoting insurgency in Kashmir. Pakistan also provisioned the Taliban with weapons to fight the "Northern Alliance" which contests Taliban control over the country and had until recently about 7% of Afghan territory, mostly north of Kabul and in the Panshir. The Northern Alliance, while including some Pashtuns, has been commanded by Ahmad Shah Massud, an ethnic Tajik. About three weeks ago, Massud was assassinated by suicide bombers identified as part of Bin Laden's group.

The bonds between Mullah Omar, and Usama Bin Laden, are bonds of blood and Bin Laden has offered "bayat" to Mullah Omar, an offering of submission to his will and his leadership. Bin Laden recently declared Taliban-ruled Afghanistan as the "new Mecca" and Mullah Omar as the new caliph. It is therefore all but impossible for Mullah Omar to turn over Bin Laden to the U.S. for prosecution as the U.S. has demanded. The Taliban and Bin Laden's estimated 4,000 to 5,000 fighters are intertwined with the Taliban military and Mullah Omar considers Bin Laden as his right hand.

What is al-Qaeda? The Arabic word means the "Base," or "foundation." Bin Laden does not refer to his international network as al-Qaeda. This word refers to his companion in arms at his headquarters in Southern Afghanistan. In his camps perhaps 10,000 Bangladeshi, Pakistani, Tunisian, Moroccan, Algerian, Egyptian and ethnic Chechens, Dagestanis, Kosovars and dozens of other nationalities have been trained.

Some of them are provided specialized intelligence training, some schooled in the arts of making improvised explosive devices, and others given instruction in the production and use of chemical weapons. Those not chosen for specialized tasks are given combat training and either sent back to their native countries to foment insurgency against their secular regimes or enlisted in his combat brigade that fights alongside the Taliban against the Northern opposition. For the past four years, Bin Laden's men have fought with the Taliban against Massud, and have suffered the losses of at least seven hundred to a thousand men in the fighting, including one of Bin Laden's own sons about seven months ago.

It is important to distinguish between the so-called "loose networks" of affiliated groups, and the tightly controlled inner circle of al-Qaeda that conceives and implements their strategic operations. The bombing of the USS Cole, for example, was a tightly controlled al-Qaeda operation that had some local support, drawn from the Islamic Army of Aden, a radical Islamic group in the Yemen set up by Bin Laden's brother-in-law and funded by Usama. The operation was apparently directed by Muhammad Atef, an Egyptian who serves as Bin Laden's Chief of Operations. It was Atef's daughter who married one of Bin Laden's sons last May, a marriage that also symbolized the merger of the Egyptian Islamic Jihad into al-Qaeda, and a new name for the inner circle: "Jidad al-Qaeda."

The Ahmad Ressam case, was an example of the use of affiliated groups by al-Qaeda to promote violence against America. This was the "millennium" plot frustrated when Ressam panicked at the Canadian/US border while transporting materials for five bombs. Ressam, a member of an Algerian terrorist faction funded and supported by Bin Laden, was trained at an al-Qaeda camp in Afghanistan and given $12,000 seed money. He was told to raise the rest of the monies needed through criminal activity in Canada, organize his cell, and choose targets in America to destroy. Ressam planned to plant bombs at Los Angeles International Airport, to kill as many people as possible. At the same time, a more centrally controlled and sensitive al-Qaeda operation was being implemented in the port of Aden, against the USS Sullivans, the sister ship of the Cole. The explosives laden boat sank in the harbor while being piloted by the two would-be suicide bombers. They swam back to shore, and went to ground, certain that their abortive operation would be discovered. It was not. About 8 months later, the same operation, using more sophisticated and lighter explosives, was carried out against the Cole. The devastating results are well known.

How does the al-Qaeda organization fund its worldwide network of cells and affiliated groups? Several businessmen in Saudi Arabia and in the Gulf contribute monies. Many of these contributions are given out of a sense of Islamic solidarity. But much of the money is paid as "protection" to avoid having the enterprises run by these men attacked. There is little doubt that a financial conduit to Bin Laden was handled through the National Commercial Bank, until the Saudi government finally arrested a number of persons and closed down the channel. It was evident that several wealthy Saudis were funneling contributions to Bin Laden through this mechanism. Now, it appears, that these wealthy individuals are siphoning off funds from their worldwide enterprises in creative and imaginative ways. For example, orders may be given to liquidate a stock portfolio in New York, and have those funds deposited in a Gulf, African or Hong Kong bank controlled by a Bin Laden associate. Other channels exist for the flow of monies to Bin Laden, through financial entities in the UAE and Qatar. Cash, carried to intermediaries, is also a source of funding. There are some female members of Bin Laden's own family who have been sending cash from Saudi Arabia to his "front" accounts in the Gulf. I will stop my remarks here, and I am prepared to address any questions you may have.

DOCUMENT 6

On October 3, 2001, the Committee on International Relations of the U.S. House of Representatives met to consider the threat posed by al-Qaeda. Oliver Revell attributes to bin Laden several attacks we now know he did not carry out. These statements and the transcript of the entire meeting may be found at http://www.international relations. house.gov/archives/107/75562.pdf

PREPARED STATEMENT OF OLIVER "BUCK" REVELL, FORMER ASSOCIATE DIRECTOR IN CHARGE OF INVESTIGATIVE AND COUNTER-INTELLIGENCE OPERATIONS, FEDERAL BUREAU OF INVESTIGATION

Chairman Hyde, I thank you and members of your Committee for the opportunity to testify during these hearings. Yours is an extremely important responsibility and I know that you and your colleagues want to provide the very best support that you can to our President and those in our Government, military, intelligence, diplomatic and law enforcement that must face this challenge. I will try and provide you with my honest and forthright assessment and opinions based upon the forty years that I have now been involved in this arena.

The terrible events of September 11, 2001 shall ever remain in our collective memories. I like so many other Americans lost friends in the attacks. I wish that I could tell you that the attacks could not have been anticipated and that we are unlikely to face such devastation again. I cannot. For it is very clear that we have been the targets of a sustained campaign of terrorism since 1979. The fall of the Shah of Iran and the establishment of a fundamentalist Islamic State in Iran under the Ayatollah Khomeini, and the invasion of Afghanistan by the Soviet Union in 1979 were the predicates of the tragedy that we suffered on September 11th. In Iran the Islamic extremists found that they could take and hold Americans hostage without serious repercussions. Out of that experience the Iranian back Hezbollah bombed our Embassies in Beirut twice and Kuwait once, as well as killing over two hundred Marines in a suicide truck bombing. The Hezbollah took American's hostage and hijacked our airliners and yet we seemed impotent to respond. Before we even knew of Osama bin Laden, Imad Mugniyah of the Hezbollah was the leading terrorist against America. He was directly responsible for the attacks against our personnel and facilities in Lebanon and yet he and his organization have never been punished for their crimes against our nation.

This example was not lost on the founders of al Qaida, primarily members of the Afghan mujahidin from Arab countries. Osama bin Laden and his associates' experienced first hand that guerilla warfare and terrorist tactics could defeat a "Super Power". He learned from Mugniyah that America was not likely to fight back. Since the attack on the American Special Forces on a humanitarian mission in Somalia in 1992 bin Laden and his associates have carried out a steady and increasingly deadly campaign against America and Americans. The following are but the publicly known events:

1. Somalia 1992
2. World Trade Center, New York, 1993
3. Planned attacks against multiple targets in New York in July 1993
4. Planned assassination of Pope John Paul in the Philippines 1994 (Americans were in the Pope's entourage)
5. Planned assassination of President Clinton in the Philippines 1995
6. Planned bombings of 11-13 American Airliners over Pacific Ocean 1995
7. Car bombing of U.S. military mission in Riyadh, Saudi Arabia 1995
8. Truck bombing of U.S. Air Force housing area Khubar Towers, Dhahran, Saudi Arabia 1996
9. Truck Bombing U.S. Embassy, Kenya 1998
10. Truck Bombing U.S. Embassy, Tanzania 1998
11. Plot to bomb Los Angeles International Airport, Y2K, New Year 2000
12. Plot to bomb East Coast target, Y2K, New Year, 2000
13. Plot to attack U.S. Naval Ship in Yemen, January 2000
14. Suicide boat attack on USS Cole, Yemen October 2000

By September 11th we certainly should have known that we were the principal targets of a terrorist campaign unlike any we had ever faced. And yet we totally failed to recognize the impending disaster that stalked our nation. Some of us in the Counter-terrorist business tried to warn of the danger, but we were generally thought of as alarmists. For the purpose of lessons learned I am citing the concerns I, among others, expressed about our lack of preparedness for the struggle we now face as a war.

In a speech to a conference held by the National Institute of Justice in May of 1999 on "Terrorism & Technology: Threat and Challenge in the 21st Century" I pointed out my concerns for our lack of readiness to deal with the growing threat of terrorism. Some of these remarks are set forth below.

"The rather abrupt end to the Cold War was expected to bring about a substantial improvement in international cooperation, and a concordant change in the manner in which governments dealt with transnational issues such as terrorism and organized crime. However, the expected improvements in overall safety and security of U.S. citizens and interests have not materialized except at the strategic level. Terrorism remains a constant and viable threat to American interests on a global basis even though the sources of the threat may be evolving into heretofore unknown or undetected elements/organizations.

The threat is changing and increasing due to the following factors:

1. The philosophy, motivation, objectives and modus operandi of terrorists groups both domestic and international has changed.
2. The new terrorist groups are not concerned with and in many instances are trying to inflict mass causalities.
3. Terrorist groups now have ready access to massive databases concerning the entire United States infrastructure including key personnel, facilities, and networks.
4. Aided by state sponsors or international organized crime groups, terrorist can obtain weapons of mass destruction.
5. The Internet now allows even small or regional terrorist groups to have a worldwide C3I (Command, Control, Communication and Intelligence) system, and propaganda dissemination capability.
6. Domestic anti-government reactionary extremists have proliferated, and now pose a significant threat to the Federal Government and to law enforcement at all levels. Militia organizations have targeted the Federal Government for hostile actions, and could target any element of our society that is deemed to be their adversary.
7. Islamic extremism has spread to the point where it now has a global infrastructure, including a substantial network in the United States.

Terrorism has been a tough political, analytical and operational target for years. Nonetheless, twenty years ago, analysts could agree on several "tenets of terrorism." First, terrorists were viewed as falling into one of three categories: those that were politically motivated, and used violence as a means to achieve legitimacy, such as the IRA or PLO, or; those that used violence as a means of uprising, or finally; those that were state-sponsored whose violence was manipulated by foreign powers to achieve political leverage. Second, terrorists were generally thought to calculate thresholds of pain and tolerance, so that their cause was not irrevocably compromised by their actions.

While U.S. officials worried about terrorists "graduating" to the use of weapons of mass destruction, especially nuclear, we believed that most terrorist groups thought mass casualties were counterproductive. This was because mass casualties seemed to de-legitimize the terrorists' cause, would certainly generate strong governmental responses, and erode terrorist group cohesion. In essence, we thought a certain logic and morality line existed beyond which terrorist dared not go. The different types of terrorist groups had a wide range of motives. The extreme left's motivation for violence has been significantly diminished by the disenchantment with communism on a global scale. These groups find that their message is out-of-fashion, and they can no longer mobilize the public to their causes. This loss of motivation is a major reason for the recent downward trend in international terrorist incidents, as documented in the State Department's report, "Patterns in Global Terrorism." The threat level of all leftist groups globally, once rated high, is now considered moderate. Of the twenty-two known groups, three have denounced violence altogether. Indeed, high collateral casualties are inconsistent with the fundamental message of leftist terrorists who profess their goal to be the betterment of the masses.

State-sponsored terror has seen a notable decline in the last several years for three primary reasons. First, the Middle East peace process has given previously violent groups and states a motive to refrain from terrorism in order to gain leverage and bargaining power at the table. Second, post Cold-War geopolitical realities have brought about many new agreements and growing cooperation among nations in countering terrorism. One of the largest sponsors of terrorism in the past—the former communist East European countries—are now aggressively supporting counter-terrorism initiatives.

However, several state sponsors remain who continue to fund, motivate, support, and train terrorists. Iran is by far the most active of these state sponsors, with the greatest long-term commitment and worldwide reach. Iraq remains of concern, but has a more limited transnational capability. However, attacks within Iraq's own backyard, such as the attempted assassination of former President George Bush in 1993 during his Kuwaiti trip, and the assassinations of dissidents in Jordan, are more likely to threaten the peace and stability of the region. Syria is a more pragmatic sponsor, by providing supplies in transit, but has refrained more recently from terrorism in order to enhance its negotiating position in the peace talks. Its loss of USSR patronage has meant a decline in financial and logistical support, but it nevertheless allows some rejectionists to maintain headquarters in Syria. Hezbollah still receives supplies through the Damascus airport and operates openly in parts of Syria and Syrian controlled territory. The newest sponsor on the list is Sudan, which was added in 1993 because of its provision of safe haven and training for a variety of terrorist groups. Sudan has hosted Osama Bin Laden's facilities. Libya, a notorious state sponsor, has also refrained lately from terrorism in order to obtain some sanctions relief. It continues, however, to target dissidents, fund extremist Palestinians, and provide safe haven for Abu Nidal, all while attempting to avoid accountability for the PanAm 103 bombing. The recent surrender of the PanAm 103 suspects came only after crippling sanctions by the United Nations. For state-sponsored terrorism, the value of deterrence retains credibility, and America should not relinquish this capability.

Radical Islamic groups are now the most active in terms of the rate of incidents. Many of these groups are considered separatists, and desire a seat at the recognition and negotiation table. Others, considered extreme Islamic zealots, operate as loosely affiliated groups, as in the World Trade Center and East African bombings. For these groups deterrence has less effect. And in fact many have stated that they wanted to maximize casualties to punish the United States, which they have demonized as the Great Satan.

Ethnic separatist terrorism, as old as mankind, can be temporarily sidetracked by a few contemporary geopolitical developments, but generally, it is impervious to such developments because its root-cause is invariable long-lived. Most of these groups seek world recognition and endorsement; to date, they have not resorted to the use of weapons of mass destruction. . . .

The argument has been made that while traditional terrorism—in terms of motivations—is still a large segment of the terrorist population, there is a new breed of terrorist for which the old paradigms either do not apply at all or have limited application. These groups—cults, religious extremists, anarchists, or serial killers—must be regarded as serious threats, and perhaps the most serious of the terrorist groups operating today. These "new" terrorists are driven by a different set of motivations: they seek an immediate reward for their act, and their motivations and objectives may range from rage, revenge, hatred, mass murder, extortion, or embarrassment, or any combination of these. They may desire mass casualties, or at least not care about how many people are killed in their attacks. As such, they do not make traditional calculations of thresholds of pain or tolerance within a society. These groups tend to be loosely affiliated both internationally and domestically, and may have no ties at all to state sponsorship. They change affiliations and identities as needed, and are extremely difficult to detect. Where traditional groups want publicity to further their cause, many "new" terrorists do not desire attribution; this is particularly true of the religious extremists, God knows, and will reward. Religious extremism is growing in numbers, and is not limited to the Islamic faith. While the "new" terrorist may have a variety of motivations, some single issue groups, such as, extremists in the animal rights, environmental, and anti-abortion movements, may also pose a significant threat, and can not be overlooked. Additionally, the new millennium is an important apocalyptic milestone for many religious or extremist cults. Many terrorist groups, both traditional and "new," have privatized their practices through a few standard business techniques (fund-raising, use of technology, etc.)

Also new today is the proliferation of knowledge and technology among many criminal, terrorist, and narcotics groups. Many of these groups are building skills in state-of-the-art communications, and weaponry. They are achieving new global links and support from one another in cooperative

Mohammed's sayings and deeds as recorded by his contemporaries, are another fundamental source. A third key element is the Sharia, the code of law derived from the Qur'an and the Hadith. Islam is divided into two main branches, Sunni and Shia. Soon after the Prophet's death, the question of choosing a new leader, or *caliph*, for the Muslim community, or *Ummah*, arose. Initially, his successors could be drawn from the Prophet's contemporaries, but with time, this was no longer possible. Those who became the Shia held that any leader of the Ummah must be a direct descendant of the Prophet; those who became the Sunni argued that lineal descent was not required if the candidate met other standards of faith and knowledge. After bloody struggles, the Sunni became (and remain) the majority sect. (The Shia are dominant in Iran.) The Caliphate—the institutionalized leadership of the Ummah—thus was a Sunni institution that continued until 1924, first under Arab and eventually under Ottoman Turkish control. Many Muslims look back at the century after the revelations to the Prophet Mohammed as a golden age. Its memory is strongest among the Arabs. What happened then—the spread of Islam from the Arabian Peninsula throughout the Middle East, North Africa, and even into Europe within less than a century—seemed, and seems, miraculous. Nostalgia for Islam's past glory remains a powerful force.

Islam is both a faith and a code of conduct for all aspects of life. For many Muslims, a good government would be one guided by the moral principles of their faith. This does not necessarily translate into a desire for clerical rule and the abolition of a secular state. It does mean that some Muslims tend to be uncomfortable with distinctions between religion and state, though Muslim rulers throughout history have readily separated the two. To extremists, however, such divisions, as well as the existence of parliaments and legislation, only prove these rulers to be false Muslims usurping God's authority over all aspects of life. Periodically, the Islamic world has seen surges of what, for want of a better term, is often labeled "fundamentalism." Denouncing waywardness among the faithful, some clerics have appealed for a return to observance of the literal teachings of the Qur'an and Hadith. One scholar from the fourteenth century from whom Bin Ladin selectively quotes, Ibn Taimiyyah, condemned both corrupt rulers and the clerics who failed to criticize them. He urged

Muslims to read the Qur'an and the Hadith for themselves, not to depend solely on learned interpreters like himself but to hold one another to account for the quality of their observance. The extreme Islamist version of history blames the decline from Islam's golden age on the rulers and people who turned away from the true path of their religion, thereby leaving Islam vulnerable to encroaching foreign powers eager to steal their land, wealth, and even their souls.

BIN LADIN'S WORLDVIEW

Despite his claims to universal leadership, Bin Ladin offers an extreme view of Islamic history designed to appeal mainly to Arabs and Sunnis. He draws on fundamentalists who blame the eventual destruction of the Caliphate on leaders who abandoned the pure path of religious devotion. He repeatedly calls on his followers to embrace martyrdom since "the walls of oppression and humiliation cannot be demolished except in a rain of bullets." For those yearning for a lost sense of order in an older, more tranquil world, he offers his "Caliphate" as an imagined alternative to today's uncertainty. For others, he offers simplistic conspiracies to explain their world. Bin Ladin also relies heavily on the Egyptian writer Sayyid Qutb. A member of the Muslim Brotherhood executed in 1966 on charges of attempting to overthrow the government, Qutb mixed Islamic scholarship with a very superficial acquaintance with Western history and thought. Sent by the Egyptian government to study in the United States in the late 1940s, Qutb returned with an enormous loathing of Western society and history. He dismissed Western achievements as entirely material, arguing that Western society possesses "nothing that will satisfy its own conscience and justify its existence."

Three basic themes emerge from Qutb's writings. First, he claimed that the world was beset with barbarism, licentiousness, and unbelief (a condition he called *jahiliyya*, the religious term for the period of ignorance prior to the revelations given to the Prophet Mohammed). Qutb argued that humans can choose only between Islam and jahiliyya. Second, he warned that more people, including Muslims, were attracted to jahiliyya and its material comforts than to his view of Islam; jahiliyya could therefore triumph over Islam. Third, no middle ground exists in what

Qutb conceived as a struggle between God and Satan. All Muslims—as he defined them—therefore must take up arms in this fight. Any Muslim who rejects his ideas is just one more nonbeliever worthy of destruction.

Bin Ladin shares Qutb's stark view, permitting him and his followers to rationalize even unprovoked mass murder as righteous defense of an embattled faith. Many Americans have wondered," Why do 'they' hate us?" Some also ask, "What can we do to stop these attacks?"

Bin Ladin and al Qaeda have given answers to both these questions. To the first, they say that America had attacked Islam; America is responsible for all conflicts involving Muslims. Thus Americans are blamed when Israelis fight with Palestinians, when Russians fight with Chechens, when Indians fight with Kashmiri Muslims, and when the Philippine government fights ethnic Muslims in its southern islands. America is also held responsible for the governments of Muslim countries, derided by al Qaeda as "your agents." Bin Ladin has stated flatly," Our fight against these governments is not separate from our fight against you." These charges found a ready audience among millions of Arabs and Muslims angry at the United States because of issues ranging from Iraq to Palestine to America's support for their countries' repressive rulers.

Bin Ladin's grievance with the United States may have started in reaction to specific U.S. policies but it quickly became far deeper. To the second question, what America could do, al Qaeda's answer was that America should abandon the Middle East, convert to Islam, and end the immorality and godlessness of its society and culture:" It is saddening to tell you that you are the worst civilization witnessed by the history of mankind." If the United States did not comply, it would be at war with the Islamic nation, a nation that al Qaeda's leaders said "desires death more than you desire life."

ANNOTATED BIBLIOGRAPHY

PRIMARY SOURCES

Abdullah Azzam

Azzam, Abdullah. *Defense of Muslim Lands, The First Obligation of Faith.* 1979. Available in translation at: http://www.islamistwatch. org/texts/azzam/defense/chap3.html

Azzam, Abdullah. *Join the Caravan.* 1988. Available in translation at http://www.religioscope.com/info/doc/jihad/azzam_caravan_5_part3.htm

Mullah Mohammed Omar

Omar, Mullah Mohammed. Interview with Voice of America. *The Guardian.* September 26, 2001. http://www.guardian.co.uk/world/2001/sep/26/afghanistan.features11

Osama bin Laden

Arnett, Peter. Interview with Osama bin Laden aired on CNN, 1997. http://www.anusha.com/osamaint.htm Arnett conducted the most comprehensive interview with bin Laden before he declared war on the U.S.

Historic Islamic Writers

al-Banna, Hasan. *Jihad*, translated at http://www.islamistwatch.org/main.html. Al-Banna founded the Muslim Brotherhood. His work inspired Osama bin Laden.

Bergen, Peter L. *The Osama bin Laden I Know*. New York: Free Press, 2006. A comprehensive anthology of statements by Osama bin Laden as well as accounts of those who knew him.

Esquire interview with Osama bin Laden, February 1999, in *Compilation of Osama bin Laden Statements, 1994-January 2004* (Washington, DC: FBIS, 2004), http://www.fas.org/irp/world/para/ubl-fbis.pdf

ibn Taymiyyah, Ahmad. *The Religious and Moral Doctrine of Jihad*, translated and excerpted at http://www.islamistwatch.org/main.html This site provides a useful translation of the teachings of the thirteenth-century Islamic Salafist, whose work inspired Osama bin Laden.

Ibrahim, Raymond, ed. and trans. *The Al Qaeda Reader*. New York: Broadway Books, 2007. This book contains a variety of al-Qaeda documents including many statements by bin Laden.

Osama bin Laden. "Bin Laden Attacks Obama Policies," Al Jazeerah English net, http://english.aljazeera.net/news/middleeast/2009/06/200963123251920623.html

Osama bin Laden. "Declaration of War against the Americans Occupying the Land of the Two Holy Places," In *Al Quds Al Arabi* [news paper published in London], August 1996, http://www.pbs.org/newshour/terrorism/international/fatwa_1996.html

Osama bin Laden. "Jihad against Jews and Crusaders," February 23, 1998, http://www.fas.org/irp/world/para/docs/980223-fatwa.htm

Osama bin Laden. "Open Letter to Sheik Abdul-Aziz bin Baz on the Invalidity of his Fatwa on Peace with the Jews," translated by the Counter Terrorism Center, U.S. Military Academy, West Point, wikisource. org/wiki /Open_Letter_to_Shaykh_Bin_Baz_on_the_Invalidity_of_his_Fatwa_on_Peace_with_the_Jews.

Qutb, Sayd. *Milestones*, originally published in 1964; translated at http://www.islamistwatch.org/texts/qutb/Milestones/characteristics.html. Qutb developed al-Banna's ideas further. He is probably the single most influential Islamist writer of the 20th century.

United Kingdom Government Document

Report of the Official Account of the Bombings in London on 7th July 2005. London: Her Majesty's Stationary Office, 2006.

U.S. Government Documents

Obama, President Barack. Transcript of Cairo University Speech. June 4, 2009. http://www.whitehouse.gov/the_press_office/Remarks-by-the-President-at-Cairo-University-6-04-09/

Report of the 9/11 Commission (Washington, DC: Government Printing Office, 2004), http://www.9-11commission.gov/report/911Report.pdf

United Nation Documents

UN Office on Drugs and Crime, *World Drug Report 2009,* http://www.unodc.org/unodc/en/data-and-analysis/WDR-2009.html

UN Security Council Document, S/RES/1054 (1996), 26 April 1996, http://daccessdds.un.org/doc/UNDOC/GEN/N96/107/86/PDF/N9610786.pdf?OpenElement

SECONDARY SOURCES

Books

Cassidy, Robert M. *Russia in Afghanistan and Chechnya: Military Strategic Culture and the Paradox of Asymmetry.* Carlisle Barracks, PA: Strategic Studies Institute, U.S. Army War College, 2003. A succinct summary and analysis of these two conflicts.

Coll, Steve. *The Bin Ladens: an Arabian Family in the American Century.* New York: The Penguin Press, 2008. This work is the only comprehensive study of the bin Laden family available in English.

Denny, Mathewson. *An Introduction to Islam.* Second edition. New York: Macmillan, 1994; 1st ed., 1985. This concise but thorough work provides an excellent overview of Islam accessible to non-academic readers.

Esposito, John. *Unholy War: Terror in the Name of Islam.* Oxford, UK: Oxford U. Press, 2002. Esposito challenges Bernard Lewis' thesis that a clash between Islam in the West has developed because of the failure of Muslim civilizations to modernize.

Gunaratna, Rohan *Inside Al Qaeda: Global Network of Terror*. New York: Columbia University Press, 2002. Gunaratna has produced what may be the best

Kepel, Giles. *Jihad: In Search of Political Islam* translated by Anthony F. Roberts. Cambridge, MA: The Belknap Press of Harvard University Press, 2002. Keppel provides a detailed account of the rise of political Islam and advances the controversial thesis that the movement is waning.

Korem, Dan. *Rage of the Random Actor*. Richardson, TX: International Focus Press, 2005. Korem exams what motivates individuals to engage in extreme violence such as terrorism.

Naylor, Sean. *Not a Good Day to Die: The Untold Story of Operation Anaconda*. New York: Penguin, 2006. Naylor is extremely critical of the conduct of this military operation.

Riedel, Brian. *Search for Al-Qaeda: Its Leadership, Ideology, and Future* (Washington, DC: Brookings Institute, 2008. Riedel served as a senior CIA Middle East analyst.

Scheuer, Michael. *Through Our Enemies' Eyes: Osama bin Laden, Radical Islam, and the Future of America*. Washington, DC: 2007; first ed., 2006. Scheuer was a long-serving CIA officer.

Stern, Jessica. *Terror in the Name of God: Why Religious Militants Kill*. New York: Harper Collins, 2003. Stern provides an excellent examination of the roots of religiously motivated terrorism.

Wright, Lawrence. *The Looming Tower: Al-Qaeda and the Road to 9/11*. New York: Alfred Knopf, 2006. Wright presents an interesting analysis of the events leading to 9/11.

Zuhur, Sherifa. *A Hundred Osamas: Islamist Threats and the Future of Counterinsurgency*. Carlisle Barracks, PA: Strategic Studies Institute, 2005. This excellent study situates Islamist extremism within the broader Islamist movement and challenges some of the basic assumptions upon which the Global War on Terror has been based.

Articles

Buchanan, Michael. "London Bombs Cost Just Hundreds." BBC Online. January 3, 2006. http://news.bbc.co.uk/2/hi/uk_news/4576346.stm

"Bundestagwahl im Visier von al-Qaieda." *Die Welt*, Sunday. July 5, 2009. p. 4.

Comas, Victor. "Al Qaeda Financing and Funding to Affiliate Groups." *Strategic Insights*, IV, no. 1 (January 2005). http://www.ccc.nps.navy.mil/si/2005/Jan/comrasJan05.asp

"The CIA's Intervention in Afghanistan," *Le Nouvel Observateur*, Paris, 15-21 January 1998, http://www.globalresearch. ca/articles/BRZ110A.html

Starkey, Jerome. "Drugs for guns: how the Afghan heroin trade is fuelling the Taliban insurgency," *The Independent* (UK). April 29, 2008. http://www.independent.co.uk/news/world/asia/drugs-for-guns-how-the-afghan-heroin-trade-is-fuelling-the-taliban-insurgency-817230.html

"World's poor drive growth in global cellphone use," *USA Today*, March 2, 2009. http://www.usatoday.com/tech/news/2009-03-02-un-digital_N.htm

Web Sources

Deobandism, Global Security, http://www.globalsecurity.org/military/intro/islam-deobandi.htm This site explains a principal sect of Islamism in South Asia.

Haykel, Bernard. "Radical Salafism: Osama's Ideology," 2001, http://muslim-canada.org/binladendawn.html#copyrightauthor The author teaches Islamic Law at New York University.

Internet World Status, http://www.internetworldstats.com/stats.htm The site provides excellent world demographic data.

MIPT Terrorism Data Base, http://www.terrorisminfo. mipt.org/incidentcalendar.asp. This site provides the most comprehensive terrorist database of terrorist incidents available.

Nasr, Seyyed Hossein Prof. of Islamic Studies, George Washington U., "Spiritual Significance of Jihad," http://www.islamicity.com/articles/Articles.asp?ref=IC0407-2391 Nasr provides a succinct, useful explanation that dispels myths about jihad.

Pew Charitable Trust, *Global Attitudes Survey*, 2004, http://pewglobal.org/reports/display.php?ReportID=206 The annual global attitudes survey provides a wealth of information on trends, beliefs, ideas, etc. around the world.

"Saudi Arabia: A Brief History." http://www.mideastweb.org/arabiahistory.htm. The Mideastweb provides useful information and sources on a wide range of topics relevant to the Middle East.

"Soviet War in Afghanistan," http://www.absoluteastronomy.com/topics/Soviet_war_in_Afghanistan The site provides some useful background information.

INDEX